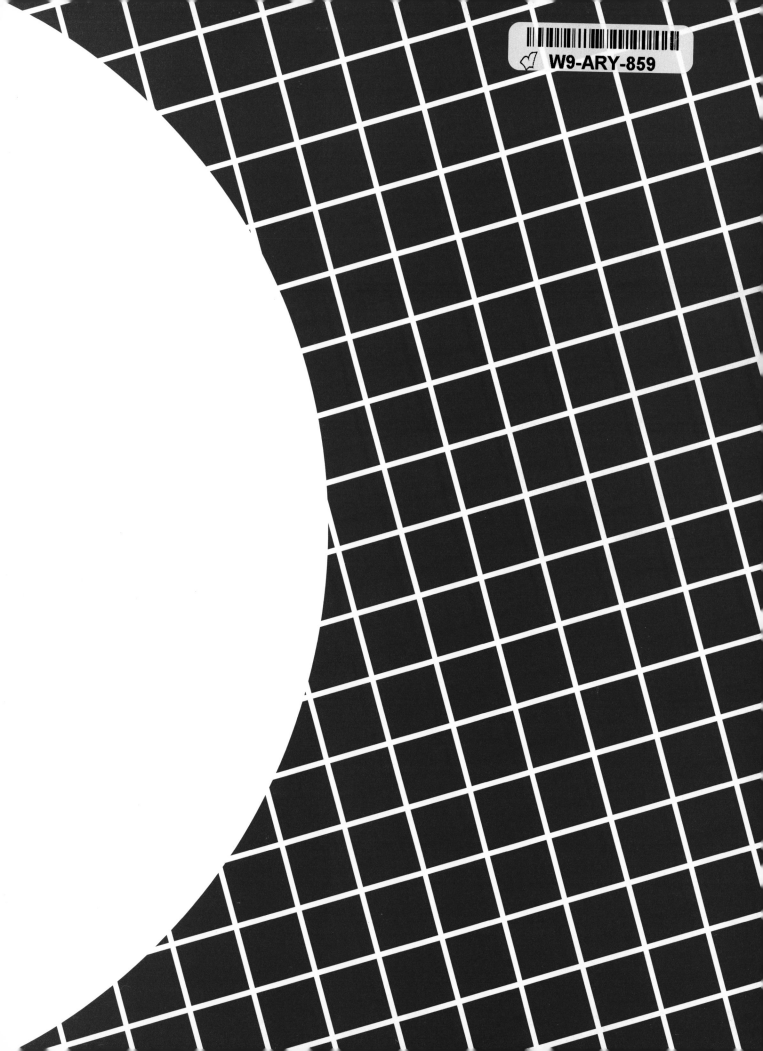

"I will write my life as. . . if it were a love story, for who shall say it is not? It began with my great love of football and it will end the same."

Ferenc Puskás, "Puskás on Puskás"

"A national football team represents a way of being, a culture."

Michel Platini, World Cup 1998 director and former captain of the national team, to L'Equipe

SOCCER!
THE GAME
AND
THE WORLD
CUP

FRANCE 98
COUPE DU MONDE
© 1994 ISL TM

U S SOCCER®
© US SOCCER 1991

Foreword by
ALAN I. ROTHENBERG
Edited by
JIM TRECKER
and
CHARLES MIERS
Design by
MIRKO ILIĆ

Essays by
SEAMUS MALIN,
ELIO TRIFARI,
RIGOBERTO
CERVANTEZ,
MARIANNE
BHONSLAY,
and
STEVE GOFF

With
KASEY KELLER,
CLAUDIO REYNA,
EDDIE POPE,
ERIC WYNALDA,
CARLA OVERBECK,
VINNIE MAURO,
TONY DICICCO,
and
STEVE SAMPSON

UNIVERSE
PUBLISHING
in association with
UNITED STATES
SOCCER
FEDERATION

First published in the United States
of America in 1998 by Universe Publishing,
A Division of Rizzoli International Publications, Inc.,
300 Park Avenue South, New York, New York 10010

98 99 2000/10 9 8 7 6 5 4 3 2 1

Library of Congress Catalog Card Number: 97-60144

Design: Mirko Ilić Corp.
Printed in the United Kingdom

Front cover: Claudio Reyna (J. B Whitesell, ISI); Kasey Keller (Ben
Radford, Allsport); Ronaldo (J. B. Whitesell, ISI); Alessandro del
Piero (J. B. Whitesell, ISI); Alan Shearer (Ross Kinnaird, Allsport)

Page 1: Italy's Roberto Baggio, 1994 (BTS, Popperfoto)
Pages 2-3: USA team vs. Mexico, 1998 (Simon Bruty,
Any Chance?) Pages 4-5: Newcastle United fans,
1997 (Mike Hewitt, Allsport) Pages 6-7: USA's
Marcelo Balboa vs. Mexico, 1998
(Doug Pensinger, Allsport)

TABLE OF CONTENTS

EDITORS' NOTE	12
FOREWORD Alan I. Rothenberg	15
FIELDS OF GREEN Seamus Malin	16
WORLD SOCCER Jim Trecker	22
THE WORLD CUP 1930–1998 Jim Trecker	42
DESTINATION FRANCE 1998	69
MAJOR LEAGUE SOCCER	76
LATIN LESSONS Rigoberto Cervantez	81
FAIR PLAY AND FOUL with Vinnie Mauro	88
KEEPING GOAL with Kasey Keller	101
CONTROLLING THE GAME with Claudio Reyna	109
DEFENDING YOUR TURF with Eddie Pope	119
GOAL SCORING with Eric Wynalda	125
ROMÁRIO AND RONALDO	130
WOMEN'S SOCCER Marianne Bhonslay	149
MIA HAMM: THE WORLD'S BEST PLAYER with Tony DiCicco	156
TEAM USA with Carla Overbeck	161
TACTICS with Steve Sampson	166
SOCCER STATS	171

A melée in the 1996 European Champions
League Final, in which Italy's Juventus
defeated Holland's Ajax Amsterdam.

(Shaun Botterill, Allsport)

A game for all
seasons: a 1997
European Cup
Winner's Cup match
100 miles above the
arctic circle, between
Norway's Tromso and
England's Chelsea.
(Gary Prior, Allsport)

Raising a storm: USA fans in Portland, Oregon, before the crucial 1997 World Cup qualifying match vs. Costa Rica.
(J. B. Whitesell, ISI)

EDITORS' NOTE

Just a short time ago, perhaps 15 years at most, soccer fans in the United States were "underground" types, forced to scour out-of-town newstands for international publications or to huddle around static-laced shortwave radio transmissions to follow the world's game. Nowadays, soccer is blossoming, fulfilling the hearty predictions made by the game's devotees in the '70s and '80s. Soccer abounds on American television outlets in English and Spanish, major networks air nearly every game played by the national team and by the clubs of Major League Soccer, and via the Internet everyone can keep up-to-date daily on the most obscure events from the farthest corners of the world. American newspapers devote more and more space to the game, certainly a legacy of the love affair struck between soccer and dozens of journalists during the 1994 World Cup. For those who follow the game passionately, today's information explosion is a welcome situation. There is no such thing as too much for a soccer fan.

But the greatest benefit to all the newfound publicity is that soccer is now exposed to millions of Americans who previously had ignored or overlooked the game. Though children have been playing the game for years, many parents perhaps had no real idea of just how universal and lovely soccer is; they had no way to view the game in a global setting. Those days are now over. National team games regularly attract crowds of 40,000 and up, MLS average attendance figures are the envy of most every league in the world, and such exciting young players as our own Reyna as well as the world's Ronaldo, Denilson, Del Piero, Vieri, Beckham, Raul, Oliseh, and West are becoming known here and can be the role models for aspiring American players.

"*Soccer: The Game and the World Cup*" has been published by the U. S. Soccer Federation in collaboration with Universe Publishing as a homage to the U. S. national teams, to our athletes—men and women—and to the beauty of the game itself. The World Cup in France in the summer of 1998 is the perfect platform to celebrate ours and the world's game.

We have searched the USA and the world for some of the finest authors to tell soccer's story, and the publishing effort has truly been global. On behalf of the countless people involved, let me especially thank Ilaria Fusina, Abigail Wilentz, Karen Ngai, Belinda Hellinger, and Elizabeth White at Universe/Rizzoli and Elio Trifari and Franco Rubis at Italy's prestigious *La Gazzetta dello Sport* newspaper. Mirko Ilić's creativity and So Takahashi's tireless work made the final product the beauty that it is.

Without photos, the ballet-like elegance of soccer would be impossible to capture. And without the work of Bob Thomas, Ian Southwell, Gary Shaeffer, and Andrew Wrighting from Popperfoto, Elena Motetti at Richiardi, Simon Bruty, and Lee Martin, Marc Glanville and Mark Trowbridge from Allsport, we could not have told the story. Our very special thanks to J. Brett Whitesell of International Sports Images, the photo manager for U. S. Soccer, who lent days of his busy career to assisting this project and whose images are invaluable.

From U. S. Soccer, much of the writing was handled flawlessly by National Team's Communications Manager Jim Froslid and Women's National Team's Press Officer Aaron Heifetz, whose insights into the players and the game bring immediacy to the player essays. Likewise, Dan Courtemanche and Trey Fitzgerald of Major League Soccer provided invaluable support to the project.

The soccer literature shelves are filled with quality works in all languages, many of which served as inspirations to us in preparing this volume. We recommend some recently published titles: Simon Kuper's *Football Against the Enemy* and *Perfect Pitch,* Pete Davies's *I Lost My Heart to the Belles* and *All Played Out,* Hugh McIlvanney's *On Football*, Nick Hornby's incomparable *Fever Pitch*, and, for the traveling set, Peterjon Cresswell and Simon Evans's *Rough Guide to European Football.*

We hope our book, like these, helps to slake the thirst for more. ⚽

"Golden girl": Shannon MacMillan scored one of the most important goals in U. S. soccer history when her shot beat Norway in the 1996 Olympics semifinal, revenging the team's 1993 World Cup loss and setting up a final encounter with China.

(J. B. Whitesell, ISI)

America's game: soccer at grass-roots level, in Richmond, Virginia, 1997.
(J. B. Whitesell, ISI)

International soccer is a magical drama of skill, unparalleled athleticism, and, above all, passion—on and off the field. Every four years the planet is captivated by the greatest single sporting event—the World Cup finals. In 1994 the eyes of billions of soccer fans were riveted on World Cup USA and now in 1998 we turn our attentions to France '98, where the United States national team will compete with 31 other top national teams for team sports' ultimate prize.

In the 1990s soccer has truly become the dominant world sport. Television coverage saturates the airwaves, newspaper space devoted to soccer has grown exponentially, and FIFA itself, the world governing body, now has more members than the United Nations. Dr. João Havelange, who ends his 24-year FIFA presidency following the 1998 World Cup, has frequently said that soccer's power is such that the sport can often accomplish what the most savvy diplomats cannot. And the 1990s have given ample proof of that: North and South Korea made quiet sounds of reconciliation during the early planning phase for the 2002 tournament to be staged in Korea and Japan; Lebanon, once a war-ravaged nation, has again hosted international matches; the tragic scenes from the Balkans occasionally soften to allow soccer matches between Bosnians, Serbs, and Croatians to take place peacefully (with Yugolsavia and Croatia both sending talented teams to the finals in France); and South Africa's joyous triumph at home in the 1996 African Nations Cup gave the emerging nation so much to be proud of.

Yes, soccer is a passionate game. We are very lucky in the United States to have had a front row seat for so many of soccer's recent memories. We are one of just a dozen nations in the entire world to have qualified for all the World Cups in this decade—and our resolve at U. S. Soccer is to make sure that the tradition continues.

U. S. Soccer started out the decade united behind the principle of producing the greatest World Cup ever. Now, as we look to the future, we are all united behind Project 2010, probably soccer's most ambitious plan ever. Simply stated, the U.S. soccer community is embarking on a mission not only to host the World Cup again but to win it—in the year 2010. Only 8 years ago, we had the youngest men's team in the finals. They narrowly lost their meeting with host Italy but held their heads–and ours—high. In 1995 we reached the last 16 in the world, and then the Copa America semifinals—and in this decade our women's team has won world *and* Olympic championships.

I've had the privilege of being involved in soccer since the late 1960s, when the dueling United Soccer Association and the National Professional Soccer League were taking the first tiny steps toward growing the game. In that 30-year span I've seen first-hand that whenever soccer people get together they always put aside differences and achieve the greater goal. It's surely going to happen again.

So in this book we celebrate our game—the world's game—as well as the world's greatest stars, especially including the national teams of the United States—men's and women's. We hope you will enjoy this magnificent celebration—*and share too in the passion.* ⚽

FOREWORD

Alan I. Rothenberg
President, U. S. Soccer Federation

FIELDS OF GREEN
SEAMUS MALIN

While traveling with the national team for World Cup telecasts, it is not uncommon for those of us who like to kick the ball around to arrange a pick-up match, usually featuring one loosely affiliated team representing folks from the television production end of things against a team representing individuals from the United States Soccer Federation. This is a movable game that goes from city to city and is of deep meaning to only about 22 individuals, but one must do what one must do to keep a foot in the game.

Before a recent World Cup match at Richmond, Virginia, we proceeded to have our pick-up game the day prior to the U.S. national team performance. The field was arranged for us in the suburbs of Richmond, and when we got there and were given instructions as to where our game was, we were greeted by a sight which spoke volumes for the state of the sport in America in 1997. Descending a slight hill, there was row upon row of soccer fields as far as one could see. It reminded me very much of the parks in the suburbs of London, which I used to ride through in the double-decker bus from Heathrow Airport. I would gaze enviously across green and somewhat soggy fields all with goalposts and nets a-waiting young English boys that afternoon or the next morning. I often wondered whether the day would come when we might have such scenes to view in our own country.

As I looked across the Richmond fields, the games were proceeding noisily and enthusiastically and beside each field were two teams ready to go on as soon as the match currently under play was over. Having come to this country in 1958 and having immediately been introduced to a college game where throw-ins were replaced by kick-ins, where sliding tackles were prohibited, where the penalty area was a semicircular arrangement, and where substitutes ran in and out of the game at will, it was delightful to see that we had come to a place that was frankly unimaginable in the '50s.

Yes, the participation level is stunning and, yes, we all recognize there is also a drop-out phenomenon from kids who are in the game primarily for recreational purposes, but nonetheless the startling visual image of row upon row of soccer fields in the heart of America is one of the more powerful and emotive statements expressing the level the game has reached. It reminded me of some of my formative experiences in the game. . . .

There was no television in 1953, at least no TV on Glenn Abbey Road in suburban Dublin, where I lived, at the time approaching my thirteenth birthday. This really didn't matter because we were all raised, in that postwar era, on radio and the movie theaters. We depended mostly on radio to provide us with vital pictures when it came to important soccer matches.

I remember May 2, 1953, as if it were yesterday, because my ear was virtually glued to the radio that afternoon despite my father's futile efforts to cajole me into mowing the front lawn. I was quite simply in another world—a nearby world perhaps, separated by the short distance of the Irish Sea and 100 miles or so of terrain to Wembley. I considered myself lucky to be part of the event, and there's no question that the radio broadcast added specially to that deep-rooted passion for the game which infects many young people, particularly if the imaginative life of the mind has a place for it.

The details of the match are still quite vivid in my mind, the stunning recovery by Blackpool when down 1–3 with only 13 minutes left, the collapse of the Bolton team, reduced to 10 men through injury (in those days you were not allowed to substitute), and the Stan Mortensen hat-trick are part of the lore of the English game. The facts of the event take second place to the larger-than-life magic of one brilliantly skillful individual who inspired a generation of right footers, such as myself: Blackpool's 38-year-old winger, Stanley Matthews.

I recall my mother's dismay when she found me taking all the kitchen chairs into the backyard to copy Matthews' childhood practice of weaving his way with a tennis ball through an array of furniture. Somehow, it was the easiest of leaps to move from chairs in a garden of suburban Dublin to the lush carpet of Wembley to which all of us so passionately aspired. . . .

Years later, I befriended a Hungarian refugee in the U. S. I recall informing him of an upcoming match which would not be on TV but which he could hear by radio. As we parted, he turned to me and said, in his still developing English, "Thanks for the information, I will watch it on the radio." Somehow, I knew exactly what he meant. . . .

> "We have experienced players who fear no one—from top to bottom, I see parity." Steve Sampson, USA coach, 1998

> "Pelé called it the beautiful game, didn't he? It's a perfect game. It's a game of athleticism, a game of power and competition and strength—anybody who thinks football is just a game of deftness and touch wouldn't win. You need courage, you need steel in your make-up. But it's the control, too. . .the spontaneous things players can do, that's what's beautiful." Bobby Robson, from Pete Davies, *All Played Out*

By 1958, TV was indeed a part of our lives. A few of the middle-class families in my Dublin suburb had a black and white set; not a moment too soon, for the World Cup that year introduced us to the astonishing man known as Pelé.

I am sure that every person who saw Pelé play would be able to tell you where he or she first laid eyes on him. For those of us who were in our teenage years, the sight of this seventeen-year-old performing on the world's largest stage was truly astonishing. Here was a contemporary of ours scoring stunning goals and showing us a new level to which we didn't dare to aspire and which we all knew to be something we might never see again. After a single evening of watching the Brazil team playing in any game there was only one recourse for those of us sitting huddled in the living room watching: taking the ball and trying it all ourselves.

Crossing this elevating experience was a more mundane and somewhat threatening phenomenon of an upcoming move from Dublin to the States. I say threatening because my parents had advertised certain items of furniture for sale that they didn't wish to take across the Atlantic. To my great dismay, and to that of all the friends who depended on our TV to embrace the World Cup, the set was high on the list.

" The World Cup is. . . for the estimated two billion viewers who get up early, stay up late, cheer at the television, bay at the moon, go out and bang drums in the middle of the night because somebody scored a goal halfway around the world." George Vescey, 1998 *(New York Times)*

My parents, on those wonderful summer evenings, would go for walks and stop in for a social drink at the local pub and, upon returning, would inquire whether we had any responses to our ads. They always looked perplexed when we conspired to report no interest in the TV set. Devious as it may have been, we could not let go of these pictures from Sweden. . . .As any parent knows, sometimes for acts of a higher purpose, bending the truth a little bit is not the end of the world, at least until the end of the World Cup. . . .

Twelve years later, I witnessed the sun-splashed match in Guadalajara between England and Brazil on a big screen at Madison Square Garden. It seemed as though there were 20,000 people in the audience, of which 19,000 or more were Brazilian. The carnival atmosphere was infectious, the colors, the beating drums, the excitement level were all there in the way we've come to expect when Brazil fans convene. It was a totally absorbing celebration of the game and, in particular, of that unique interpretation which is Brazilian.

England was, of course, the defending World Cup champion. This was to be the most significant challenge in the first round and Brazil had assembled a team that was clearly every bit as good, if not better, than the 1958 team: a team to erase the memory of the

History in the making: FIFA president Jules Rimet and a young boy start the draw for the 1938 World Cup.

(Popperfoto)

abusive treatment Brazil received in the 1966 World Cup finals in England.

As the camera zoomed in on the teams, Brazilians were on their feet chanting the names of each individual player as he appeared. When the camera revealed the English players, their images were greeted with derision, whistling, laughter, and maybe even some contempt. The overall feeling was that these were goats among thoroughbreds and that this would be a virtual execution. But

"If you go to a favela [Brazil's poorer areas], you will see. . . the smartest of the boys [who] can put up a fight, is a good football player. . .There is a deep connection between tricking defenders and being a smart boy in real life."
Simon Kuper,
Football Against the Enemy

suddenly there appeared on the screen, his brow furrowed with that sense of worry that he carried, his hair thinned since 1966, of course none other than the endearing and brilliant Bobby Charlton. The reaction was extraordinary: the entire Brazilian contingent was standing, cheering, and applauding his name.

I was absolutely stunned. Here were perhaps the greatest lovers of the game expecting a Brazilian display never to be forgotten but still taking the time to pay respect to one player who might have been, in another life, Brazilian. . . .

Theater of dreams: revered English player Bobby Charlton, with teammates, Banks, Cohen, Ball, Moore, and Stiles, holds the World Cup aloft at Wembley in 1966.
(Popperfoto)

If you go to Barcelona you will learn that it is a city full of architectural wonder and enthralling museums. It may surprise you to learn that the most frequently visited museum in the city is the museum of the football club of Barcelona.

Barcelona's Nou Camp stadium is a mecca for soccer in Spain. Although it competes for such a title with the Bernabéu in Madrid, the Nou Camp is more significant because of its importance to Catalonian pride and autonomy. During the Franco years, when Catalonian ambitions were firmly repressed by the central government, the arena was the only place to express Catalonian identity. People sang their songs, they waved the colors of Catalonia, which could not be flown otherwise in public, and acted in vigorous defiance of central authority. Perhaps then it was no surprise that when the 1992 Olympics came to Barcelona, there was still evidence of the tension between the province of Catalonia and the rest of Spain.

It is well known that this antipathy often manifests itself when it comes to support for the Spanish national team. Rarely, in fact, does the team play international matches in Barcelona because there is such substantial antipathy towards the concept of Spanish nationhood in Catalonia. For the Olympics in 1992, Spain played all of its matches at venues outside Barcelona, primarily in Valencia. But for the final itself, which Spain reached undefeated, the national team had no choice but to go for the gold in the Nou Camp.

Going for the gold temporarily suspended some of the more bitter anti-national feelings, and when the team turned out to play Poland, the 95,000 gathered in the Nou Camp were

> "The meaning of FIFA is peace and unity. The world of football is different from the world of politics. Iran, the USA, Germany, Yugoslavia, we are all in the same family." Dariush Mostafavi, former Iranian federation president *(New York Times)*

> "Wherever you are there will be the diamond you'd love to take with you. . .the good player whose personality doesn't quite dovetail with your own . . . the player who gets by, but doesn't really have the talent. . .the one who has all the talent in the world but isn't prepared to maximize it—so it's about your ability to get men to follow you as a leader." Roy Hodgson to Joe Lovejoy, *The London Sunday Times*

100 percent behind the national team. But by halftime things were not looking so good, as Spain had fallen behind, 0–1, to Poland. There then occurred one of those phenomena which seemed to be a side story. . .namely the arrival in the stadium of King Juan Carlos I and his family.

The king is not a popular person in Catalonia. He had, however, gone out of his way to be sensitive to Catalonian aspirations. As he arrived, the audience applauded and simultaneously the teams came out for the second half. Almost immediately, Spain scored two goals. Poland, showing remarkable skill and resilience, then drew level two minutes from the end, and we seemed destined for extra time. . .until, in the 90th minute, just at the death of the game, Pico Narvaez seized on a rebound, steered the ball in, and the stadium erupted. The king, a great sportsman himself, was seen pumping his arms fervently.

With virtually the last kick of the game, the gold medal had been won. But the crowd's ecstasy was not just about a moment of triumph for the players, it was truly a healing moment and a vivid reminder of the power of sports to transform—a moving moment to see what sport at its best can do to bring people to a place of hope even in the midst of visceral incompatibility. . . .

Another of my most memorable experiences was when I played with a man named Chris Ohili in his sophomore year (my senior year) in college. He was a world class athlete who represented his country, Nigeria, at the Rome Olympics in 1960 in both track and field and soccer. The game I recall most vividly was not the one in which my college beat Cornell by nine goals to one, and he scored five, but rather the game in which we scored four against Amherst and had a fifth goal disallowed. He had scored all four goals. On the fifth one, the ball came swerving over my head, far too high for me even to attempt to get at, so I turned away disappointedly, but a pair of shoes went flashing by my face. I looked up and, to my amazement, there was Ohili flying through the air amidst a crowd of players. He was somehow above me and sent the ball from about 15 yards into the corner of the net.

It was a truly astonishing goal. The referee blew his whistle and disallowed it on the theory, he told us, that no player could possibly have gotten that high without leaning or pushing off an opponent. It was the decision of a philistine who obviously had no appreciation for the extraordinary talent he had just been a witness to. It was the only time in my life I would ever see our college coach literally chase a referee after a game, because, although the game was won handily, a piece of unusually striking beauty had been taken off the record book. . . . ⚽

The global game: ceremonies at the finale to the 1996 African Nations Cup, South Africa's triumphant reentry into the soccer world. South Africa's team won the championship, the country's first soccer tournament since the apartheid era ended.

(Allsport)

WORLD SOCCER

The game of soccer has been the world's most popular sport for the past one hundred and twenty-five years, whether measured in terms of countries participating (198 nations—more than there are members of the United Nations—competed in the 1998 World Cup qualifying rounds), spectators watching (it is estimated 2 billion people watched the last World Cup), or in terms of the approximately 200 million players who participate in organized leagues and associations. Remarkably, as we stand at the edge of the next millennium, there are yet new forces capable of extending the game into the new age—now making it a truly global sport.

Soccer in the twenty-first century will be global because in the 1990s soccer's governing body, FIFA (Fédération Internationale de Football Association), realized several profound manifestations of its world view.

In 1994 the World Cup was hosted by the United States, a benchmark for U.S. expansion and development of the game as well as for global development, as this was the first time the world's most popular and prestigious sporting contest had been held outside Europe and Latin America. Major League Soccer, now a twelve-team professional men's league, was spun off that 1994 event, completing a remarkable growth cycle in America that had begun with the 1960s youth soccer boom and the pioneering North American Soccer League, the first professional North American league.

In keeping with this geographic expansion of the game, FIFA-organized youth championships have spurred rapid development of top-class soccer in Asia and Africa. The proof is in the expanded slate of qualifiers for the World Cup finals, now open to 32 qualifying nations, with a special emphasis on including more teams than before from those two continents. In World Cup terms, bearing in mind the intense national pride attached to reaching this final stage of the tournament, African representation has skyrocketed, from two teams to five, in just 12 years. Asia was guaranteed three spots plus a chance for a fourth qualifier in the France tournament for 1998, twice what was available just one cup earlier.

Potentially the most important development for genuinely spreading the sport globally in the long run is not found in geographic selection but rather in gender representation: two FIFA Women's World Championships were staged (1991, China; 1995, Sweden) and a third was assigned to the United States for 1999. So fast is the growth of the women's game that the third World Championship will be a 16-team affair.

In the 1990s the game has been embraced as never before by a worldwide communications revolution. Soccer on television is a global staple: FIFA's World Cup remains the crown jewel, but it seems that every major soccer competition, from the lucrative European Champions League to MLS Cup, is televised across the planet. While we should not overstate the American role—the United States, after all, is not yet a major soccer nation despite its tremendous youth boom and the growth of the pro game—it is certainly true that the acceptance of the game at the top level in America completes a plan fostered by longtime FIFA president João Havelange thirty years ago, a plan that successfully envisioned as rapid an internationalization of soccer in the last part of the twentieth century as was achieved in a comparable period a century earlier.

Since 1904, when FIFA was founded among seven European countries to foster international competition (Belgium played France that year in FIFA's first game), soccer's base has gradually increased: in 1913 the United States joined FIFA; in 1923 Egypt became Africa's first representative; in 1929 Japan entered; and in 1963 Australia. When Havelange succeeded Sir Stanley Rous at the head of world soccer in 1974, he accelerated the game's growth and bluntly altered its direction by looking beyond the traditional strongholds of Europe and Latin America. It was Havelange, ably assisted by FIFA General Secretary Joseph (Sepp) Blatter, who cajoled, lectured, and evangelized when necessary. Slowly the World Cup expanded and the decision to give America the host's role in 1994 proved a masterstroke. On the verge of that event there remained naysayers; in its wake, after five weeks of capacity crowds and unprecedented attention to the sport at all levels of American society, there could be no turning back. But that's where we are now. How did it all begin?

While the game of soccer has universal origins from the distant past, the modern version of the sport popular across the world owes its existence to the nineteenth-century flowering of organized sporting games in Britain's elite "public" schools.

From medieval times to the early nineteenth century in Britain, team sports had evolved that might be classified under the general names of mob football or hurling (a sport still played in more organized form with great fervor through-out Ireland and, with some variation, in Australia), in which groups of players quite aggressively tried to reach various goals—sometimes even as far away as the next village–by dribbling or running with a ball. In Renaissance Florence there was a game popular among aristocrats called *giuoco del calcio*, which somewhat resembled today's rugby, but the era of recognizable modern football began between the early and mid-nineteenth century at such exclusive British schools as Eton, Harrow, Uppingham, and Rugby, where a variety of team games gradually evolved into the codifiable and closely related sports of soccer and rugby (Eton still plays the Field Game, which could be considered a mixture of the two sports).

In 1863 graduates of these schools preferring the less physical game, in which players dribbled the ball and did not use their hands to tackle the opposition or move the ball ("fair catches" were allowed, but there were no goalkeepers, per se, for another eight years), founded the Football

Milan's Internazionale fans ("punching the air 'til it's black and blue") before a game with arch rivals A.C. Milan at San Siro, Italy's soccer mecca. Known as the soccer world's "shop window" for the talent on parade every Sunday, the stadium is home to both teams.

(David Cannon, Allsport)

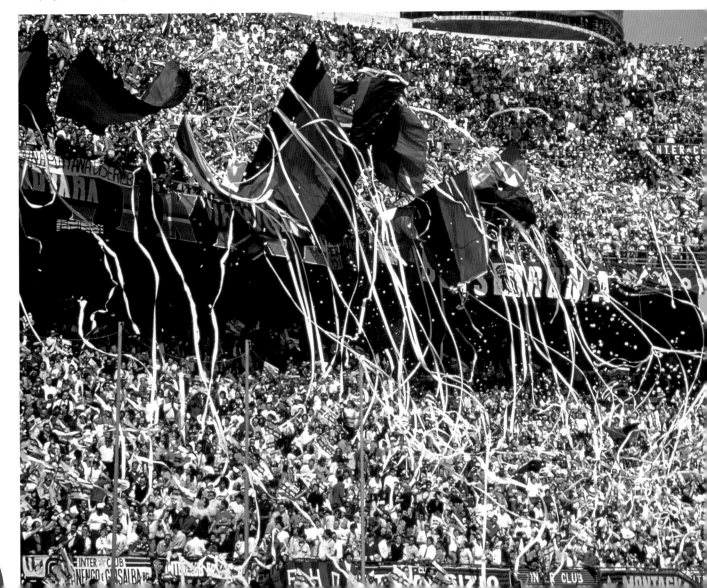

this period. The only major changes since involve the offside rule, which has been successively altered—first to prevent excessive scoring, but more recently to discourage stultifying defenses—goalkeeper play, substitution, and more technical aspects of the sport.

One of the attractive features of soccer is the fact that the game played in the 1990s is essentially the same as it was more than a hundred years before. Naturally the players of today are fitter and thoroughly professional, in contrast to the amateurs who dominated the early days, but their skills are basically the same, as is the object of the sport. That makes it possible to compare players and teams over time, a feature in which soccer is similar to baseball; in America the eternal debates about the relative worth of a Babe Ruth, Mickey Mantle, or Willie Mays is mirrored overseas in discussion of the merits of Alfredo Di Stefano, Bobby Charlton, Johan Cruyff, Franz Beckenbauer and, of course, the incomparable Pelé.

The fact that upper-class Britons went from their famous schools to establish an empire upon which "the sun never set" explains how the sport was transported across the globe in the short space of approximately fifty years. From Moscow to Montevideo, British industrialists and expatriates established clubs wherever they were posted. Between 1857 and 1867, when the first football clubs were founded (Sheffield and Hallam in England; Queen's Park in Scotland) and 1902, when the first European international match was played, between Denmark and Austria, the game spread across the world with extraordinary rapidity, being formally organized in places as far from Britain as Argentina (1867), Uruguay (1882), and the United States (1867), with Brazil (1890s), Germany (mid-1880s), and Italy (1887) relative latecomers. The sport, perhaps aided by its simplicity of rules (a Reverend Thring wrote a football rules booklet for boys at Uppingham School in 1860 entitled "The Simplest Game"), quickly took root with local people; in South America, immigrants from Europe, Italians particularly, popularized it and established their own clubs.

To this day subtle reminders of the British diaspora that so influenced the game can still be seen across the globe, not only in the formal composition of soccer's rule-making body, the International Board (founded in 1882), in which the 8 seats were long held by the four British associations (England, Scotland, Northern Ireland, and Wales still retain four seats) but also in the names of such venerable teams as Italy's Genoa Cricket and Football Club, Argentina's Newell's Old Boys (named after a British schoolmaster who introduced the game to his school), and, indeed, Major League

Association, composed of 14 footballing clubs that wanted to compete within an established set of rules. Charles Wreford Brown, a player for Charterhouse School's alumni team, Old Carthusians and Corinthians, coined the word "soccer" in abbreviating the term Association to distinguish this game from the Rugby Union's game of football (pioneered by William Webb Ellis in some form as early as 1823 at the Rugby School and codified in 1871).

If soccer started to become an organized game when it diverged from rugby in the middle of the last century, at one time both games were essentially the same, involving 15 to 20 players on each team trying to advance a ball across a goal line. In the early definition of the sport, handling the ball was widely permitted, as well as tackling in the style common to American and rugby football today. However, with the advent of sets of rules at English public schools, soccer developed as a game played without the hands and with rules limiting the types and amount of body contact.

Today's game evolved from 1860 to 1910, during which time all the important rules were enacted. The size of the playing field was established as somewhat larger than a U.S. football field, the goals were determined as 8 yards wide and 8 feet high, and the crucial decisions regarding the number of players (11) and the types of fouls were all taken during

Soccer's D. C. United, as well as in the uniforms of such clubs as Spain's Athletic Bilbao and Italy's Juventus, whose stripes are directly derived from the strip of Sunderland United and Notts County, respectively.

The English combination of a round-robin league system (begun in 1889) and the simultaneous single-elimination, knockout trophy, or cup, competitions (begun in 1871–72) is used in almost all soccer-playing countries.

Soccer took root early in the United States. Mob football was played (and periodically banned) by the early settlers. Organized football began in the 1820s at Harvard; by 1862 Oneida Football Club of Boston had been founded to follow English dribbling rules; by 1867 Princeton and Rutgers had organized teams playing a style of football, and by 1873 Yale had defeated Princeton in a game very close to soccer.

By 1876, however, rugby rules were being preferred by Harvard, Princeton, and Columbia, and with the formation of their own Intercollegiate Football Association, the foundation of today's American football was established.

PLANET FOOTBALL

Soccer's roots are truly universal, as there are reports of sports involving teams moving a ball between goals from ancient China (*tsu-chu*) and Japan (*kemari*), from the Aztecs and from the ancient Greeks (*episkyros*). Roman legionnaires are known to have played a team game called *harpastum*, perhaps closer to rugby than to soccer, that was imported into Britain and might be considered the ancestor of early mob football. Clearly, the ease and speed with which the British game spread in the late nineteenth century must be attributed principally to the human interests in collective athletic activities and in demonstrating skills with a ball, as well as to the simplicity of a game with only 14 original rules.

Thus, from the early twentieth century, the game of soccer was truly international, in terms of its participants, its organization, and its competitiveness, with such countries as Austria, Belgium, Czechoslovakia, Denmark, Germany, Holland, Italy, Hungary, Switzerland, Argentina, Brazil, and Uruguay being at various times the most successful in international tournaments and the most innovative in tactical developments as well as in strategic approaches to the sport. International games began with competition between England and Scotland in 1872, but the initial impetus for spreading international play came through the Olympics, as soccer at this level was an amateur game in many countries until after the First World War (though professionalization at the club level began as early as the 1870s). There were limited tournaments at the first three Olympiads of this century. By the 1924 Olympic Games, the sport was being contested intercontinentally at the national level, with Uruguay emerging as emphatic winners and demonstrating for the first time the prowess of South American soccer.

FIFA organized its first World Cup in 1930, an idea that followed up on the success of the 1924 Olympics soccer tournament; a succession of regional international events has come largely since the Second World War.

There are still such long-standing rivalries as Argentina–Uruguay, Austria–Hungary, Germany–France, and Italy–Switzerland, which stretch back to the start of international play. On the club level, the growth of the international game progressed more slowly, with Central European teams the first to organize and stage regular tournaments. In 1955–56, urged by the French sports newspaper *L'Equipe*, the first European Champions Cup was staged between the leading club teams (then the league winners) from the European countries, and the club game took on a new dimension. Spain's Real Madrid, led by the Argentine Di Stefano, won the cup five times, from 1956 to 1960. There have since been periods of dominance by such clubs as Ajax Amsterdam, Liverpool, Bayern Munich, Juventus, and A.C. Milan. Now there are three major European club tournaments (contested between league winners, cup winners, and other successful club teams from the previous season), a South American club championship (the Copa Libertadores), which rivals its European counterpart, and growing club tournaments in Africa, Asia, and the Central–North American and Caribbean Region (CONCACAF). There is even an unofficial world club championship between the European Cup and South American Cup winners, played each year in neutral Tokyo, as well as a growing movement to conduct a worldwide club event.

The impetus for much international growth has been television, a factor since the 1966 World Cup was staged in England. That was the first major soccer championship which could take advantage of communications satellites (though the first live World Cup broadcasts were in 1954) and even the restrictive television policies of many European nations could not prevent the rapid evolution of the game

The scrum in the Wall Game, contested exclusively on the fields of Eton College. A door and a tree by the wall are goals (though no goal has been scored since 1909!). The famed school propagated several forms of football: in 1883, Blackburn Olympic beat Old Etonians in the F. A. Cup Final.

(Anton Want, Allsport)

from spectator-based to a television-based spectacular. Almost all of the major leagues have exclusive television deals today, and rights fees for events like the European Champions League and the World Cup have become comparable to the prices demanded by American sports leagues. They have become international properties, too; Champions League games are televised live in the United States while the American professional championship game, MLS Cup, is seen live in Europe. Managing all of this is not a simple process, and soccer's organizational structure often has been perceived as complicated by Americans used to a simpler professional league format. Soccer has vitally important professional leagues, but its worldwide nature means that its governance is dominated by the global umbrella and initiatives move downward, toward the national and local level.

Most important of all soccer organizations is FIFA, which controls the game in every nation on earth. FIFA certifies national associations, usually called football associations, in each country and empowers those associations to govern the various leagues in each nation. The national football league is, thus, a member of its own F. A., which is affiliated with FIFA. The leagues themselves operate by the permission of FIFA and must abide by eligibility and rules decisions handed down from the top authority. FIFA, headquartered in Zurich, Switzerland, has survived almost as many changes as the game it supervises. The FIFA president remains the single most powerful figure in the game, but even that could change after the retirement of Havelange.

FIFA FACTS

which experimented with rules, the MLS game is the FIFA game with minor variations in time-keeping and match management (and with an experimental unique penalty shootout system to settle ties). Ties and the referee's discretionary control over when "ninety minutes" has actually been played (traditionally an excruciatingly tension-filled element in close games) are considered anathema to American sportsmanship. U. S. schools and colleges have also moved considerably closer to the world rules, although greater player partic-

ipation is still encouraged by the presence of freer substitution laws.

At the national level, each football association is responsible for producing a national team and certifying the various competitions that take place each season. The country's F.A. employs the national team coach and has the power to select players from individual clubs in order to compete in international events. Although there has long been conflict between the interests of the professional clubs, who want to win their league or cup, and the national associations, who often must draw on players mid-season for brief training and competitive international duty, FIFA has moved strongly in recent years to insure that players are always available for events like World Cup qualifying matches. This has become increasingly important as players have gained employment outside their own country and may be involved in leagues whose schedules are not all in concert.

A 1996 European Community court decision which ended soccer's traditional "reserve clause" has accelerated demands for an international calendar, regulated by FIFA. As in American baseball, the age of free-agency has meant even greater player movement; in soccer's case it is interconti-

The first known photograph of a soccer game: capped players from Aston Villa and West Bromwich Albion, still two of England's more popular clubs and local rivals, contest the 1887 F.A. Cup Final at the Oval, London. Aston Villa won 2–0.

(Gazzetta dello Sport)

The first known photograph of an international game in Europe: Italy's Genoa Cricket and Football Club and France's Nice, still both active professional clubs, play in 1893.
(Gazzetta dello Sport)

nental. World Cup matches require American players to come from their clubs in Europe to play for the USA; similarly, Argentina and Brazil find their national team players spread over the continents.

Although Americans often see world soccer only in terms of the international competitions, like the World Cup or the Olympic Games, the sport's greatest worldwide strength is at club level. Just like devout baseball fans in the United States, almost every European and South American fan passionately follows a club at the national and local level (often one and the same) and usually also is keeping an eye on a hometown player who has gone to the "big leagues," or a bigger club or another country's league, to make his fortune. Even at the highest level, clubs in many countries are literally still that: memberships of local supporters with significant fan input. Beyond that, because soccer is used as the vehicle for determining weekly lottery winners in many nations, the results of the matches are eagerly followed by a population much larger than the actual number of sports fans.

Most soccer clubs are engaged in a minimum of two competitions each year. The league championship is usually the most coveted title in Europe or South America, where teams play a fall-to-spring schedule encompassing anywhere from 30 to 44 league games. Contested like the North American National Hockey League, teams get points for a win (universally now three) or a draw (one) and none for a loss. This means that championships are decided on points rather than winning percentage. As important, the league is divided into a hierarchy. In most countries there are several divisions of teams (first division—often known by a formal name, such as Serie A, Premier, or Bundesliga—second, third, etc.), tiered according to league performance: at the end of a league season two or three teams from the top division are relegated to the second division, to be replaced by those at the top of the second division, and so forth through the divisions. This is quite unlike American sports, and creates an intense interest in the results of even the least successful teams. Occasionally a major club, such as Olympique Marseille or Manchester United, has toppled for a season or two into the second division to the aghast reactions of their legions of supporters.

In addition to the league championships, there are also national cup competitions patterned after the oldest such tournament, the English Football Association Cup. These events are knockout affairs involving clubs from all levels of the sport. The United States Open Cup, in fact, is one of the oldest tournaments of this type, begun in 1914. Whereas most professional leagues are arranged in divisions, comparable to our major league–minor league divisions in baseball, the cup tournaments may see amateur or semi-professional teams drawn against the best pros in a country. Obviously a prime attraction of such games is the possibility of major upsets; they occur with much greater frequency than might be supposed because soccer, again like baseball, is a game that is unpredictable on any single day. Even as professionalism has increased in America that tradition of cup "shocks" has been maintained; there was even an amateur team, the Bridgeport (Connecticut) Italians, in the second round of the 1997 U.S. Open Cup, while a third division side, the San Francisco Bay Seals, reached the semifinals of the same year's tournament after beating two MLS teams along the way.

Over the past 100 years, several countries have emerged as the leading practitioners of the game, with each contributing a style of play that helps to make soccer a unique sport. The game tends to be played according to the "character" and, indeed, climate of a country, so there is a marked contrast in style and attitude of players and teams. This, in part, explains the sometimes volatile nature

THE RULES

One of the beauties of soccer is that the rules of the game are simple and universal; six-year olds play the same game as professionals. One seemingly minor change took effect in 1992 and, in retrospect, it has become a hallmark of the current game. That change forbid goalkeepers to handle a ball that had been kicked back to them by a teammate. It didn't sound radical, but the effect was immediately to stop delaying tactics, to make the goalkeeper a more active field player, and to increase scoring measurably. The text said nothing about "heading" back to your own 'keeper, but that loophole will soon be closed. Another example of "tinkering" came in 1997, when FIFA instituted the "five second" rule, which requires a keeper to release the ball within five seconds of gaining control.

of the sport, which often throws together teams with quite different definitions of what constitutes a foul and whose players come from radically diverse social backgrounds. Although the British spread the game, they were not as successful in inculcating their original notions of sportsmanship and "fair play" across the globe. The result is a FIFA-inspired initiative that has been in place for a decade: the Fair Play symbol has become as prominent at FIFA events as the black-and-white checked soccer ball, itself.

The United States, not surprisingly, has turned out to be a true soccer melting pot. The 1994 World Cup proved just how many devoted fans live in this country—it being the only time almost every World Cup finals match was sold out; the state of the game in 1998 demonstrates how many play and enjoy the sport. The American soccer world now includes four distinct levels. First, the international game, a rich source of success and support. The U.S. women have won a World Cup (1991) and an Olympic gold medal (1996). They are playing before ever-growing crowds and will host the 1999 FIFA Women's World Cup in eight U.S. cities. The U.S. men reached round two (the sweet sixteen) of the 1994 World Cup and are on course to make a third straight appearance in the finals in 1998. That comes in stark contrast to the 40-year drought between the 1950 upset of England in Brazil, often considered the greatest upset in World Cup play, and the qualification for Italia '90. In 1995, the U.S. men advanced to the semifinal of the Copa America (the Americas' international championship), perhaps the strongest indication that they can be among the world's best

teams. The U.S. men now routinely sell out major stadiums for World Cup qualifying matches. A team which played in small-sized venues while qualifying for 1990 now goes to Foxboro, RFK Stadium, or the Rose Bowl and attracts capacity houses even when games are televised live.

Second, there is the professional game, which has both outdoor and indoor components. Major League Soccer, of course, is atop the American pro pyramid, but a growing number of USISL second division (A-League) and third division sides provide a proving ground for future top-level players. There are two major indoor leagues, the NPSL, which competes during the traditional winter season, and the CISL, which plays in the summer. It is widely expected that an American pro women's league will be in place soon. There is talk of starting a circuit in 1998, but U.S. Soccer is on record as preferring to defer the launch until after the 1999 World Cup.

Third, there is the school game, which grew rapidly over the past three decades, and the college game, which has burst out in remarkable fashion, especially on the women's level. NCAA Division I collegiate women's soccer is probably the best in the world; driven by player-development needs of MLS, Division I men's college soccer will probably alter its face in the immediate future, too.

And last, the youth game, the "engine room" of American

In Nairobi, young footballers improvise with balls of mud and straw. Africa joined FIFA only in 1957; in 1978 Tunisia beat Mexico in the World Cup; by 1990, Cameroon was a quarter-finalist, announcing the arrival of African soccer.

(Ben Radford, Allsport)

development. Even if it hadn't become a buzzword in the 1996 presidential elections, the term "soccer mom" would have made its way into our vocabulary. The ubiquitous presence of youth soccer players in television commercials is paralleled by the appearances of stars the youngsters can aspire to emulate, such as Mia Hamm and Alexi Lalas. The game is so firmly entrenched across the country that soccer goalposts and weekend youth games are now as integral to the American landscape as baseball diamonds and softball. For boys and girls it is often their introduction to team sports, as it is without the physical limitations, injuries, and costs of football.

The emerging game in America is now broadly shaped by European and Latin influences. The Latin nations have contributed some distinct features to the development of the international game: the practice of individual skills at the highest level, encouraged by an audience which appreciates the showmanship and the creativity of the especially audacious players; fanatical devotion to the national team, as evidenced by the old saw, "Some nations have their history, Uruguay has its soccer"; and a record of tremendous success in World Cup play. Argentina, the World Cup winner both in 1978 and 1986 and the losing finalist in 1990, is known as the birthplace of league soccer in South America. Its First Division, based largely upon the clubs in

Learning to "dribble past life's difficulties," inventing moves, such as the bicycle kick, and tricking your opponent with showmanship—these are the fundamentals of Brazilian soccer expressed on the world stage and on the beaches of Rio.

(Popperfoto)

the Greater Buenos Aires region, is the most successful on the continent, both in terms of its clubs' success in the Copa Libertadores (the South American club tournament) and its ability to lure the best players from neighboring nations to its clubs. Among the great Argentine clubs are Boca Juniors, Estudiantes de la Plata, Independiente of Avellaneda, and River Plate. Matches between Boca and River—called "super classicos" in Latin America—attract capacity crowds of 77,000 to the Monumental Stadium, the home of River Plate and the de facto national stadium. Fans in the country often follow one or the other in addition to their local team and the atmosphere inside the stadium for a match of this type is unique—even for soccer. Argentine fans, who are mimicked in neighboring Chile and Uruguay, rock stadiums as they chant and sway feverishly throughout a game, accompanied by deafening impromptu drums and bands of musicians.

Brazil has done even better than Argentina in terms of World Cup achievement, winning three times and therefore retiring the first cup, the Jules Rimet Trophy. Their victories in 1958 and 1962 were sparked by the appearance of the youthful Pelé, while the 1970 victory in Mexico City marked Pelé's final World Cup appearance and signaled the impending end of his career as the country's official "national resource." Yes, the Brazilian legislature actually made it law that Pelé could not be sold to an overseas club during his prime, the result being that he remained with Santos, a São Paulo club, throughout his Brazilian playing days. His impact on the game was tremendous as he combined uniquely acrobatic skills, brilliant playmaking, and goal scoring (1,284

goals in 1,363 games) with a tremendously positive enthusiasm for the sport. After his retirement from the top level he did, of course, come to the United States to play in the NASL with the Cosmos (a special favor to the United States formally requested by then Secretary of State and soccer aficionado Henry Kissinger), sparking a brief period of intense interest in the club and capacity crowds in Giants Stadium.

On the field, Brazil's influence on the game has been gigantic. The country's tendency to produce great individual attackers is the reason for the image of Brazilian play as creative and multidimensional, but it has always been based on the mastery of fundamental techniques. Brazilian players are masters of ball-control skills, trapping, dribbling, and heading. They first perfected, if not invented, such moves as the bicycle kick and bending a free kick around a defensive wall. They are also such excellent ball passers that the attacking moves, although spontaneous, appear choreographed. And they are masters of varying the tempo of a match, capable of taking the game from an almost walking pace to uncatchable sprinting in a split second. Where the Brazilians have not been as successful is in the matter of defensive rigor; as a result there has been a tug-of-war between those Brazilian coaches who advocate a more European style of stamina-based play and those who stress a continuation of the traditional Brazilian flair. Recent World Cups have seen teams that fell somewhere between the two schools; all failed to realize the nation's great expectations. This was particularly true of the 1982 team, which was stunned by Italy in the second round, thus missing its widely expected spot in the final. This dilemma was resolved in 1994, when Brazil put together perhaps its most complete eleven and won its fourth World Cup, in the Rose Bowl. They are favorites to repeat in 1998 because once again they have developed a genius attacker, the young Ronaldo, who labors under the pressure of comparisons to the great Pelé, but still has succeeded at two of the world's great clubs, Barcelona and Inter Milan.

Uruguay has a secure place in soccer history because it was the first Latin nation to make a vivid international statement, at the Olympic Games of the 1920s. Emerging as the top nation in the world at that time, the Uruguayans then served as hosts for the first World Cup, staged in Montevideo in 1930. They won it, then won again against the odds in Brazil in 1950. In 1995 Uruguay also won the Copa America, beating Brazil in the final at home, but they have not been important in recent World Cup play (missing the 1994 and 1998 finals). Still, they are among an elite group of once-powerful soccer nations who have retained a certain aura whenever they do field a strong eleven.

European soccer has always been known more for its variety of national styles and its adaptations to climatic conditions. Britain, of course, gave definitions to most of the game's terms and set the earliest standard for the European game, but it has been decades since British international teams have ranked at the top level. Indeed, England, considered unbeatable until the 1950s, has not fared particularly well in World Cup play, winning only once, at home in 1966 in a disputed final with West Germany ("thirty years of hurt never stopped me dreaming," goes the refrain to a 1996 popular song about following the English team). The other British "home countries" have done even less well. One can argue that qualification for the World Cup finals by small "nations" like Northern Ireland, Scotland, and Wales is achievement in and of itself, but they are minnows, not giants in the world soccer sea.

What cannot be denied is the contribution of the British club game, particularly the English Premier League. Noted for an intense, balanced competition more than for the level of player skill or the artistry of its sides, the English League was the traditional measuring stick for all soccer until very recent years. Today the Italian League is ranked the best in the world, but even that great competition is not as evenly balanced or fraught with as many challenges as an English club faces over a 38-game league season (plus cup competitions). Because of the varied weather and heavy rainfall in Britain, clubs must be able to play both the ground game and the aerial game in order to succeed. And because the British public—to say nothing of an often acerbic media—demands obvious all-out physical commitment from the players, the level of intensity in English games may be unmatched anywhere.

The great English clubs—Arsenal, Chelsea, Liverpool, Manchester United, to name just four—are known even in areas like the United States, where soccer is not so well-reported. They have been giants for nearly a century. The same is true for the Glasgow pair of Celtic and Rangers, rivals not only in soccer but in sectarian matters; Celtic is a Roman Catholic club with links to the Republic of Ireland; Rangers a Protestant club firmly embraced by United Kingdom "unionists," including supporters of Northern Ireland. (The sectarianism extends to the field; Rangers did not knowingly sign a Catholic player until 1989.). Their head-to-head matches (known as Old Firm derbies, for the longevi-

SOCCER'S COSMOS

In 1968 two rival leagues (NPSL and USSA) merged to form the North American Soccer League (NASL). The New York Cosmos franchise was formed in 1971 and was an upset winner of the league in 1972. The real coup came in 1975, when the Cosmos elevated professional soccer in America to unprecedented levels of interest and play by signing Pelé, who had retired from his national team in 1971 and was transferred from his club, Santos, for a fee of $4.5 million. In 1976, the Cosmos built on that success by signing Italian national team forward Giorgio Chinaglia from Lazio. World Cup and international stars Franz Beckenbauer, Johan Neeskens, and Carlos Alberto Torres were among many foreign players then brought to the team, which won five league titles, from 1977 to 1982.

ty of the rivalry) are some of the most hotly contested in the world; their fans exchange a stream of religious and political taunts from opposite ends of the stadium irrespective of the action on the field. To say there is nothing like it in American sports is to understate the case.

While Britain is known for competition and commitment, Germany, Italy, and the Netherlands have made greater tactical contributions in the era since the Second World War. Germany, the most consistently successful European team in the world, has organized coaching and player-development to a high degree; Italy perfected a great league structure that took the game into the modern era of huge salaries, highly talented squads of interchangeable stars (many from other countries), technical perfectionism, and adventurous marketing. The Netherlands has consistently produced coaches and players whose ideas and techniques have introduced tactical innovations into the late twentieth-century version of the sport.

Germany rose to prominence despite the scars of the war, surprisingly winning the 1954 World Cup, then organizing a national league, the Bundesliga, which replaced the older, less efficient regional structures of the game. The result was a burst of energy and enthusiasm which saw German soccer develop into the European juggernaut. Starting in 1966, the Germans' World Cup record is nothing short of amazing:

1966, runner-up; 1970, semifinalist; 1974, winner; 1978, beaten second round; 1982, runner-up; 1986, runner-up; 1990, winner; 1994, quarterfinalist. Germany is also the current European champion, having prevailed over the Czech Republic with international soccer's first "golden goal" (a sudden-death decider) in the 1996 final. (One might also footnote that the German team has not lost a penalty shootout in fifteen years.)

Along the way the German player Franz Beckenbauer, nicknamed "the Kaiser," redefined the entire concept of defense, taking the position of centerback from a strictly defensive posture to one of calculated counterattack and playmaking. There was such an abundance of talent on German fields in the 1970s that the European club tournaments came to be dominated by the achievements of Bayern Munich, Borussia Moenchengladbach, SV Hamburg, and others. At that time, the Bundesliga was the acknowledged world pace-setter.

Italy overtook Germany in terms of league strength when it reopened its border to foreign players in the 1980s (after a ten-year prohibition), a move that coincided with the arrival of Italian television as a major force in the sport. While other European countries had rigid controls on TV—often state-supported networks were the only available fare—Italy experimented with private television as early as the late 1970s, when Silvio Berlusconi, today the head of A.C. Milan, the country's top club, began broadcasting from Koper, Croatia, then part of Yugoslavia. Sport was a major lure, and soccer, from just about anywhere in the world, a keenly looked-to feature of the independent broadcasts. Suddenly Italy learned what America, especially the NFL, had already discovered; soccer could be a hot market property, a vehicle for advertising revenues undreamed of a decade before. Thus, flush with new money, the big Italian clubs cornered most of the world's top talent and spurred the development of European-wide soccer in partnership with television.

It is often argued that competition between the world's big clubs will someday overtake the World Cup itself in popularity and a worldwide television-driven club tournament could rival the

PEN TO PITCH

Orwell frowned on soccer's nationalistic vision, but Camus wrote of the formative experience of playing goal in his youth. Roddy Doyle has written avidly about following the Irish team. Nabokov, Priestley, and Pinter have also waxed about the game. A rich vein was tapped in 1991 by Nick Hornby's *Fever Pitch*, a seminal book on the highs and lows of being a fan, which empowered other fans to feel their word was invaluable, too. More unusually, Jorge Valdano, goal scorer for Argentina in the 1986 World Cup Final, is a published author of fiction.

world championship of FIFA. That remains to be seen.

The contributions by the Netherlands revolved mainly around the great Ajax Amsterdam side created by Stefan Kovacs in the early 1970s and pushed to later brilliance by Louis van Gaal (now at Barcelona) in this decade. By having players master several positions and allowing them the freedom to interchange at will, Kovacs introduced the "total soccer" approach to the game that Holland's 1974 World Cup team made famous in its run to the final. Although the Dutch

did not win that title (and again were beaten in the final by hosts Argentina in 1978), few argued that they weren't the most effective side in a tournament that also included a very strong German championship team and a wonderfully well-balanced Poland, the first strong Eastern European eleven since the Hungarian national side of the 1950s.

Total soccer has not been embraced by everybody, but most of the world's top clubs understood immediately the

need for players of versatility and exceptional physical condition. Today's defenders must be as skilled as the attackers when it comes to shooting and ball control, the forwards as effective as the backs in terms of man-to-man marking. It is no longer sufficient for a player to depend entirely on one aspect of his game in order to fit into a side. Even someone as gifted as Argentina's Diego Maradona had to become a much more complete player when he joined first Barcelona, then Napoli, in the early 1980s.

The success of the U.S. women's national team is founded in collegiate soccer. North Carolina, with 15 national championships in the past 17 years, is a dynasty unique in college sports, but recently has been challenged by Notre Dame, 1995 NCAA Dvision I champions.

(J. B. Whitesell/ISI)

The latest change in the club game came from the European Court ruling which ended the soccer reserve clause in the European Economic Community. The once-insular English league, for example, has become home to many of the world's great stars, as a television-driven expansion of revenues has turned the Premier League teams into some of the world's most prominent. Rebuilt stadia and the infusion of world-level talent into the Premiership has returned the English clubs to the highest level and appears to have sharpened the English national team, as well. The great clubs of Spain, Italy, and England, and Holland, Germany, and France, to a lesser degree, now vie for the best players in the world, drawing on the reservoirs of all European, South American—and North American—and African talent to create thoroughly international squads.

Eastern European soccer history has two distinct phases. In the early days of the developing world game, nations like the former Czechoslovakia and Hungary demonstrated an ability to create outstanding players and clubs as well as international teams, but there was not the range of European competition to showcase them. After World War II, when the Soviet Union absorbed the East European nations as a part of the Communist bloc, great emphasis was put on the Olympic Games. In soccer this meant that the full-time players from all of the old Soviet satellites were often competing against western amateurs. The result was Communist domination of the gold medals and western devaluation of Olympic soccer.

The Soviet Union, itself, has to take some credit for organizing the game in Eastern Europe. By transporting its comprehensive youth system to other countries, the Soviet influence doubtless helped the development of better club soccer in Bulgaria, Romania, and Yugoslavia. The Czechs, Hungarians, and Poles already had great soccer traditions, but the advent of teams from Bulgaria and Romania that could compete on equal terms with the West was noteworthy. In the 1994 World Cup it was Bulgaria that created one of the great stories, eliminating Germany in a Giants Stadium quarterfinal, then extending finalist Italy to the limit before eventually finishing fourth. Hristo Stoichkov was one of the stars of the competition.

Strangely, Soviet soccer itself did not achieve the lofty goals that the commissars set for it. Olympic success was attained, but the USSR never won a World Cup despite having several contending teams. It was argued that the USSR system, which subordinated individual players to a larger team concept, was not capable of crossing the gap between the creation of merely good teams and great ones. Even the attempt to piggy-back the national team onto the dominant Soviet club side of the last two decades—Dynamo Kiev of the Ukraine—did not work. Although Dynamo supplied almost all of the national team players, the result was not greater international cohesion but rather the exhaustion of players, pressed for both club and national team duty.

Hungary, of course, is noted for having turned out the best-ever Eastern European team. The Magic Magyars of 1951–54 achieved immortality by ending England's seventy-year unbeaten home record and then set up an international performance record which may never be beaten. Their totally unexpected upset loss to West Germany in the 1954 World Cup Final ended a three-year unbeaten run. What might have turned into a Hungarian dynasty did not materialize because of radical political change within the country two years later. Because the great Honved-Budapest club, with most of the national team players in its side, was on an overseas tour at the time of the 1956 Hungarian uprising, many of the players—including the great Ferenc Puskás—defected and never again wore their national team shirts.

The NCAA men's game is played by 675 colleges. As in basketball, relatively small institutions (such as 1996 finalists Florida International and St. John's) can be as competitive as such major universities and perennial powers U.C.L.A., Virginia, and Indiana.

(J. B. Whitesell, ISI)

The advent of Africa as a soccer force is a post–World War II phenomenon that follows the pattern of colonial emancipation. North Africa, with its English and French influences, was the first to produce competitive national teams. Algeria owns one of the great upsets in World Cup play, a victory over West Germany in the 1982 World Cup, while Morocco has qualified for three World Cup finals and even won its first round group in the 1986 tournament in Mexico. Tunisia qualified for the 1998 finals after finishing as African Nations runner-up in 1996. Egypt, the most populous North African soccer-playing nation, finally qualified for the 1990 World Cup finals after several near misses. Its influence has been much greater at the club level, where Egyptian clubs have been front-runners in the various continental tournaments.

Black Africa made its first appearance in a World Cup final in 1974 when Zaire qualified for the tournament in West Germany. The team made little impression, however, and it was not until Cameroon arrived on the scene in 1982 that

soccer in the sub-Saharan region was taken seriously. The political ban on South Africa undoubtedly slowed the growth of African soccer, because the sport is tremendously popular in that country, especially among the large black population. But isolation from the world game because of the ruling body's apartheid policies meant that South African promise was not realized until 1996, when the country hosted, and won, the African championship. They have now qualified for their first World Cup and promise to add a dimension to the tournament in France.

Cameroon, however, has proved so powerful that FIFA recognized their quarterfinals-reaching achievement of the 1990 World Cup by awarding Africa a third qualifying place for the 1994 competition. Further African success in 1994 increased that allotment to five places for 1998 and the Indomitable Lions duly gained their place by qualifying for a third consecutive finals.

Along with Cameroon, Ghana and Nigeria—at the FIFA world youth level—have also made the breakthrough to the top, while only the tragic air crash of April 1993, which robbed Zambia of many of its top players, has put that

country's soccer development future into question. Nigeria, which won the 1994 African title and reached the World Cup second round, has conclusively demonstrated its right to a place among soccer's powers by winning the 1996 Olympic gold medal. The Nigerians beat strong teams, close to World Cup finals level, from Brazil and Argentina to achieve that milestone and will head to France as one of the tournament favorites.

The development of soccer in the other FIFA regions, Asia, CONCACAF, and Oceania has been more uneven. Currently East Asia is poised to grow most quickly because of the serious interest shown in China, Japan, and South Korea. China emerged from international soccer isolation in the early 1980s, while both Japan and South Korea have developed fully professional leagues, which are bound to raise their level of talent. Japan and South Korea will co-host the 2002 World Cup, further boosting the game.

In addition, the growth of soccer in the wealthy Persian Gulf states contributes to the basis for Asia's future. Kuwait, Saudi Arabia, and Qatar have already made the mark in international youth competitions, while Iran and Iraq both have strong soccer histories and the potential to produce powerful national teams. A history of civil and military strife in the region has made growth problematic, but it appears that greater stability in the region will produce increased soccer interest and international success.

CONCACAF, which comprises the North and Central America–Caribbean region, has been the least successful of the large organizations under the FIFA umbrella. In part this can be explained by the relatively small populations in many of the member nations (only Mexico and the United States are populous countries), but there is also the history of the area, as soccer has never been a major sport outside Mexico. The firmly entrenched American professional sports dominate in Canada and the United States, while much of the Caribbean has taken greater interest in cricket (and baseball) and track and field than in soccer. As a result, despite the occasional strong performance from Central American representatives like Costa Rica, El Salvador, and Honduras, there is little pedigree at the international level. That is changing, however. Along with the growth of the game in the United States, the emergence of Mexico as a regional power, successful as a "guest" nation in three visits to Copa America, accompanies the rise of Caribbean teams from Jamaica and Trinidad and Tobago.

Oceania, which plays off with an Asian team for a 1998 World Cup spot, is essentially Australia and the rest, although New Zealand did qualify for the 1982 World Cup in Spain. Australia, like the United States a melting pot of diverse ethnic groups, has recently begun to compete effectively at the international level thanks to hosting two world youth tournaments. Soccer, however, still lags well behind two forms of rugby and the indigenous Australian Rules Football (a close relation to hurling and old forms of football), all of which outdraw soccer for fans and for the services of many of the top athletes.

American youth soccer participation has virtually doubled over the past decade—in 1997 a record 3.2 million children registered to play soccer, either with U. S. Youth Soccer, the American Youth Soccer Organization, or the Soccer Association for Youth.

(J. B. Whitesell, ISI)

34

Soccer has truly become a heartland sport, with Utah, Kansas, Delaware, Missouri, and Iowa boasting the highest rates of soccer participation. Showing consistent growth in every state, soccer is now recognized as the youth sport with the most players engaged in scheduled league competition.

(J. B. Whitesell, ISI)

Although there is great variety in approach across the globe, one aspect of soccer seems universal: it is an easy game to learn to play and one which provokes passionate spectator response. The fact that nationalism has been grafted onto a game that is emotionally stirring at most competitive levels has helped to turn the international soccer field into a highly charged arena. The World Cup has become the biggest sporting event on the globe, dwarfing the Olympics in terms of television audience and year-round interest. When it decided to award the 1994 World Cup to the United States, FIFA was both self-serving and idealistic. On the one hand, the world body hoped to be able to tap into an American sports marketplace which is not only rich, but potentially larger than any single European country. If the game could be successfully established in the USA at the professional level, everyone from FIFA, to the players, to the clubs stood to benefit.

In 1988, when FIFA chose the USA, many felt there was little likelihood of that happening. The USA had not outwardly embraced soccer, except at the recreational youth level, and there had been no demonstrated correlation between youth success and eventual professional popularity. Those who argued that soccer was bound to succeed because of the numbers of children playing the game were told to study the history of softball or swimming before waxing so optimistic. But there was another facet of the American story which should have been noted: soccer is the only sport in the United States which has virtually equal participation among both boys and girls. The fact that women play such a prominent part in American soccer became a focus of the 1996 Olympics, perceived as the "break out" event for international women's sport.

The naysayers were proven completely wrong when Major League Soccer launched, also in 1996. Carefully planned and orchestrated to secure financial backing and long-term commitments, MLS had actually delayed its launch a year. When it appeared as America's fifth major professional team sport, live attendance and television audiences exceeded everyone's expectations. Even a second-year dip in attendance did not seem particularly negative; the average of better than 14,000 spectators per game was 2,000 ahead of projections at the time of launch.

FIFA's idealism has been rewarded: soccer advocates are vindicated in their belief that the game can sell itself anywhere if presented in the proper way. The World Cup, the kind of mega-event that usually manages to catch the attention of even the least interested Americans, was that showcase. The big payoff is just now being realized. ⚽

D. C. United captain John Harkes holding his team's second MLS Cup, after the 1997 2–1 victory over the Colorado Rapids.
(Simon Bruty, Allsport)

Opening day for MLS, 1996: San Jose Clash and D. C. United at Spartan Stadium. United lost 1–0, but claimed the trophy 6 months later.
(J. B. Whitesell, ISI)

SOCCER'S PRIZES

J. B. Priestley referred to the "Iliads and Odysseys" that characterize the winding road of a long season. No league had greater parity in 1996 than the new MLS—but D. C. United is now its fledgling dynasty. In 1997 the 1996 runners-up, L. A. Galaxy, and D. C. United added to their season the CONCACAF Champions Cup, finishing second and third, respectively, to Mexico's Cruz Azul, while the Dallas Burn beat D.C. United for the U.S. Cup on penalty kicks. This full season, plus internationals, now replicates the game's overall program. The soccer world has a precise, orderly structure of international and club championships, cups, and tournaments, but one that offers myriad riches to those who have "stretched out and grasped their ambition." ⚽

F. C. Schalke's Olaf Thon celebrates winning the 1997 UEFA Cup over Milan's Internazionale. Played on a home-and-away aggregate score basis, qualification is based principally on high league position the previous season.
(Ben Radford, Allsport)

Germany's Jürgen Klinsmann receives the quadrennial European Championship trophy from Queen Elizabeth II, after defeating Czech Republic, 2–1, in 1996.
(Shaun Botterill, Allsport)

Cup Final day is a royal occasion in England: Prince Charles and Princess Diana present the famed F. A. trophy to Tottenham Hotspur's Gary Mabbutt in 1991.
(Bob Thomas, Popperfoto)

After beating Brazil, Mexico's Jorge Campos and Marcelino Bernal parade the 1996 CONCACAF Gold Cup, an invitational event contested every 2 years among the region's national teams.
(David Leah, Allsport)

Borussia Dortmund's Jürgen Kohler with the 1997 Champions League trophy after defeating holders Juventus, 3–1. Contested by the previous season's league winners and runners-up, the cup has been won by Real Madrid 6 times, followed by A. C. Milan with 5.
(Shaun Botterill, Allsport)

Symbolizing the new "internationalized" club, Dutch coach Ruud Gullit's all-star cast of Italian, French, Romanian, Norwegian (and even British) players took Chelsea to a 1997 victory over Middlesbrough in England's most prestigious tournament, the F.A. Cup.
(Ben Radford, Allsport)

All South Africa celebrated the 1996 African Nations triumph. F. W. De Klerk and President Nelson Mandela presented the trophy to Neil Tovey, after the home team beat Tunisia, 2–1.
(TempSport, Richiardi)

Juventus' Alessandro del Piero and Angelo Peruzzi after defeating River Plate, 1–0, to win the 1996 World Club championship, contested since 1960. A.C. Milan, Peñarol, and Nacional have each won 3 times; Borussia Dortmund beat Cruzeiro in 1997.
(Anton Want, Allsport)

Romania's Gica Popescu lifts the 1997 European Cup Winners Cup for Barcelona, after a 1–0 win over Paris St. Germain.
(Stu Forster, Allsport)

Uruguay's Enzo Francescoli with the Copa America after defeating Brazil, 2–1, in 1995: the trophy is contested by South America's national teams—and CONCACAF invitees—every two years (and was won by Brazil in 1997).
(David Leah, Allsport)

World Cup–winner, as a player and later as a
coach, Franz Beckenbauer exults after winning
soccer's ultimate prize for West Germany in 1974.

1930

The first World Cup was not nearly so glamorous as its modern-day equivalent. In fact, the competition got off to a rather inauspicious start. Uruguay was awarded the tournament (over bids from Italy, Holland, Spain, and Sweden) because its soccer authorities promised to pay European teams' expenses and to build a new stadium in the intervening eight months. Also, it was Uruguay's 100th anniversary of independence.

However, European teams were reluctant to travel such a long way and after much discussion and pressure only four teams decided to accept the invitation to participate. King Carol of Romania began a long tradition of political intervention in team selection by picking his nation's team personally. More to the good, he was instrumental in helping to salvage European participation in the 1930 tournament. This was the only World Cup in which qualification rounds were not played: Belgium, Yugoslavia, France, and Romania sailed for Montevideo, joining the USA, Argentina, Chile, Mexico, Bolivia, Brazil, Paraguay, Peru, and the hosts.

Stadio Centenario, Montevideo, in 1930, held 100,000 fans. The largest stadiums are Rio's Maracaña, holding 203,849, São Paulo's Morumbi, and Saudi Arabia's Rey Fahd (120,000 fans saw the 1998 World Cup qualifying match vs. Iran).

(Gazzetta dello Sport)

Despite promises to have Stadio Centenario ready, it was not available for the inaugural game, which was relegated to a club stadium. The teams from France and Mexico contested the first World Cup game on 13 July 1930, at Pocitos, with the French, led by forwards Alex Villaplane and Alex Thépot, winning emphatically 4–1.

In Group One, Argentina struggled against the French, before winning 1–0, then thrashed Mexico and Chile to reach the semifinals. Several matches were controversial. In the game against the French, the referee blew his whistle after only 84 minutes and was forced to call the teams back to the field for the conclusion after he realized and admitted his error. Against Mexico, the referee, Mr. Saucedo of Bolivia, awarded the Argentines five penalty kicks in the 6–3 win, greatly easing Argentina's path.

THE WORLD CUP
1930–1998

Yugoslavia surprised Brazil, 2–1, on goals by Aleksandar Tirnanic and Ivan Beck, while Uruguay and the United States raced to the semifinals without surrendering a goal.

Argentina and Uruguay, both strong favorites, did the expected in the semifinals, ending the runs of the United States and Yugoslavia by identical, 6–1, scores. For Uruguay, the victory put the team in its third straight "world championship" final, since the team had won the previous two Olympic Games tournaments, in 1924 and 1928.

The World Cup reached a dramatic conclusion with the final. Uruguay and Argentina were traditional rivals, having played 97 times previously, including a 2–1 Uruguayan victory in the 1928 Olympics final. The tension increased enormously in the three days between the semifinals and the final as waves of Argentine fans flocked to the wharfs seeking boats to ferry them across the River Plate to the game.

For their part, the citizens of Montevideo were urged to exercise maximum vigilance against the passionate Argentine fans, so that "no Argentine guns can penetrate the stadium," as one newspaper headlined. Stadio Centenario had its capacity reduced for security reasons and troops with fixed bayonets ringed the outside perimeter.

Despite this air of confrontation, however, the game itself was held without incident, under the direction of Belgian referee John Langenus. With goals by Pablo Dorado, Pedro Cea, Santos Iriarte, and Hector Castro, Uruguay handily took the title, 4–2. Even the great Guillermo Stabile could not raise Argentina to the necessary level to offset the talented and carefully coached Uruguayans.

Argentina, claiming their fans were brutally treated, broke off soccer relations with their Uruguayan counterparts following the match and refused to play them for several years. But the competition had laid the foundation for FIFA president Jules Rimet's dream of a global World Cup. Despite some dubious refereeing, the tournament did produce quality soccer and confirmation of Uruguay's role as one of the game's world leaders. ⚽

THE SURPRISING STAR

Although Argentina did not win the first World Cup, forward Guillermo Stabile was certainly a dominant figure of the games. Nicknamed "El Filtrador," for his speed and canny knack of penetrating defenses, Stabile scored 8 goals to lead the tournament. He first was a member of Argentina's national team in 1926, but came to the World Cup as a reserve. Only when Roberto Cherro was sidelined with a "nervous disorder" did Stabile have a spot in the first eleven. He began his career with Argentina's Huracán club, before his World Cup performance attracted attention in Europe. Genoa purchased him following the tournament, but injuries kept him from reaching his full potential. He ultimately played for Napoli and then Red Star in France before becoming Argentina's national team coach and leading them back to the World Cup finals in Sweden in 1958. He died on December 27, 1966, a legend both in Europe and Argentina. ⚽

USA PLAY

The United States provided some humor and some significance to the 1930 World Cup. Trainer John Coll was involved in one of the tournament's lighter moments when he raced onto the field to treat an injured player during the semifinal against Argentina. When the referee asked him to leave, the diminutive Coll argued so energetically that his bag of medicines fell to the ground, shattering a vial of chloroform. Enveloped in the fumes, Coll immediately felt faint and had to be led from the field.

The USA's team's tactical approach to the tournament was among the most sophisticated of the times, a noteworthy achievement considering the fact that the team had never played together prior to the tournament. With "huge men with enormous thighs," as one opponent put it, the team essentially lined up eight defenders and three attackers. This formation was revolutionary, in a time of high goal scoring and cavalier attacking, and foreshadowed the 1960s, when defensive-oriented soccer, known as *catenaccio*, after the Italian club and national teams who perfected it, took over the game. ⚽

1934

Thirty-two nations entered the second World Cup as the roots to the tournament deepened significantly. Instead of a tournament by invitation, the event now required qualification games, so FIFA organized 12 groups of teams in Europe, North/Central America, and South America to determine among themselves the final participants.

When the teams assembled in Italy, it became clear that the expectations of the ruling Italian Fascist party, who saw the tournament as a propaganda showcase for their government, and the home team's drive to win would become major elements of the tournament. Uruguay wasn't present, choosing to return the snubs it had received from European teams in 1930, the only time in history that the World Cup holder has failed to defend its title. But Italy's squad, under coach Vittorio Pozzo, and Austria's "Wunderteam," coached by Hugo Meisl, were there and considered favorites.

Pozzo, though not sympathetic to Fascist philosophy, did prepare his team in a manner that made it clear they wanted to win at nearly any cost. He held extended training camps that were military in nature and theory. Austria, however, took quite the opposite approach. Meisl had inspired a team that competed with immense grace and style—a team that enchanted fans for many years because of its freely expressive spirit.

The tournament was played in a knockout format right from the start: one loss and a team was eliminated. But not until the quarterfinals did this World Cup gain any particular flavor and then it was not particularly pleasant, either. Brawling and physical violence became the trademark of the round. Austria snuck by Hungary, 2–1, but Italy and Spain battled, literally, to a 1–1 tie, Spain surviving due to the heroics of Spanish goalkeeper Ricardo Zamora. Seven Spaniards and four Italians were injured in the mayhem and did not suit up the following day for the replay—then the only method of breaking a tie. Giuseppe Meazza's header after 11 minutes saved Italy's home-team hopes in the replay, which by all reports was a surprisingly civil match between the surviving players.

In one semifinal, Czechoslovakia, behind the outstanding work of Oldrich Nejedly (2 goals), Rudolf Krcil (1 goal), and goalkeeper Frantisek Planicka, ousted Germany. The other semifinal paired the teams most thought deserved to be in the final: Italy and Austria. June 6, 1934, brought rain to Milan and muddy conditions to San Siro Stadium. The heavy field conditions stymied the elegant Austrians, and Italy's Luis Monti negated Mathias Sindelar, Austria's scoring star. Italy won, 1–0, behind Enrique Guaita's goal.

In the final, in Rome, the Czechs' neat, short passing game looked invincible against the less creative Italians. Antonio Puc scored after 70 minutes; but the fleet Orsi tied the game 10 minutes later to send the tie into overtime, the first extra-time game in World Cup history. With 30 more minutes to play, the Italians' strict training methods and conditioning were influential. Just five minutes after the start, Angelo Schiavio, a center forward from Bologna, scored on a magnificent curving shot that Planicka lunged at but couldn't reach. Schiavio said later that he had only "the strength of desperation" to take the shot, but it was sufficient to give Italy the World Cup, 2–1.

With 250 journalists watching from the stands, Mussolini, Italy's Fascist leader, presented the medals. Later that day he invited the entire Italian team to his residence for a reception, posing with them for press photographs. Italy's delegate to FIFA remarked that "every one of our guests felt the throbbing of the masculine energies, of a bursting vitality, in this our Mussolini's Italy."

A further dark shadow crept into the third-place match when Germany's team arrived for the medal ceremony with two flags, one the traditional black, yellow, and red German colors and the other a Nazi banner.

But despite the unfortunate political overtones, the World

Cup was a success. It was a tournament of such great goalkeepers as Giampiero Combi of Italy, Peter Platzer of Austria, and Zamora and Planicka. Sadly, because of politics, it was the Austrian Wunderteam's only appearance on the global stage. ⚽

DICTATING THE GAME

Vittorio Pozzo was "kind, but with a strong hand," as he said about himself. Despite an authoritarian streak as a coach, Pozzo had the necessary flexibility to handle the egocentric Italians and Argentines who formed his national team. (Beginning a strategy used universally, most recently by coaches seeking to improve the Irish and Jamaican national teams, the Italian federation stretched World Cup nationalization credentials to the allowable limit by combing the globe for the best players with Italian parents, finding many of them in South America.)

Pozzo held isolated training camps, where he instilled in his players a powerful sense of work ethic and sacrifice. Some later commentators have questioned Pozzo's methods, wondering aloud if it was soccer or war that he was preparing for. Nevertheless, he ultimately earned a hallowed place in soccer history as the only person to coach two World Cup champions.

Completely consumed by soccer, Pozzo was a player as a youth, then became a journalist, and finally a soccer coach. He took over the Italian national team on December 1, 1929, and remained at his post until August 5, 1948. ⚽

THE WUNDERTEAM

Austria's Wunderteam may not have won the 1934 World Cup, but Hugo Meisl's squad remains one of soccer's greatest teams. Occasionally called upon to defend his creative, pass-oriented tactics, Meisl stood by his theories even with disappointing results in the 1920s. Meisl and fans worldwide were rewarded, however, when the Austrians' finesse and skill took them to the World Cup. Players such as center forward Mathias Sindelar, Karl Seszta (a wrestling champion who took to soccer later), and winger Karl Zischek, known as "the Ghost," all brought immense technical skills to the team. They had beaten Italy in three of the previous four confrontations, including a game in February 1934. But the World Cup semifinal loss and the Anschluss, the forced joining of Austria and Germany, spelled the end of Meisl's Wunderteam. ⚽

The 1938 World Cup in France was marked by outstanding center forwards and the power of Vittorio Pozzo's rebuilt Italian team.

The tournament continued to grow, now embracing 36 entrants, who played qualification games for 12 months to determine the 15 finalists. It was mainly a European affair, as Argentina said no and Uruguay, still angry over the lack of European participation in 1930, refused to participate. Only Cuba and Brazil came from the Western Hemisphere.

But war was perhaps the most important pre-tournament theme. Spain was engulfed in its civil war and Austria had already been annexed by Germany. Depriving the World Cup of the Wunderteam, Germany fielded a "pan-German" team, using some of the Austrians.

Nevertheless, the World Cup was a success. Pozzo brought only two of his 1934 champions to the tournament. Notable among the new names was Silvio Piola, a center forward who was tall and strong in the air. Joining Piola as attacking stars in the tournament were Dr. György Sarosi of Hungary, Leónidas of Brazil, the first black star to play for his country, and Ernest Wilimowski of Poland, each of whom achieved fame over the 15-day span of the World Cup.

Italy opened shakily, barely beating Norway 2–1 in overtime, thanks to two Piola goals. Norway hit the post three times, but Italy was through to the quarterfinals of the knockout formula tournament. Surprisingly, Cuba joined Switzerland, Czechoslovakia, Hungary, France, and Sweden as quarterfinalists. Brazil, too, reached the quarterfinals, but only after a remarkable 6–5 extra-time game, which became a personal showdown between Leónidas and Wilimowski. Each of them had four goals, a single-game record for an individual scorer that still stands. Italy's hard edge returned against France in the next round, as Piola added two more goals in a 3–1 victory in Paris. The same round's Brazil–Czechoslovakia match, held to inaugurate the new Bordeaux stadium, was a disgraceful affair, ending 1–1. Nejedly suffered a broken leg, goalkeeper Frantisek Planicka a broken arm, and four players were

At home in Paris and in Rome, where he starred for Lazio, Italy's Piola (light shirt) puts the first of his two goals beyond Hungary's Szabo in the 4–2 Italian victory in the 1938 World Cup Final.

(Gazzetta dello Sport)

sent off by the Hungarian referee. For the replay, two days later, only 7 of the original 22 could suit up. Leónidas and Roberto scored and the 1934 finalists were out.

The semifinals featured the first meeting in history between two of soccer's great nations: Italy and Brazil. For reasons which remain controversial today, Brazil's manager, Ademar Pimenta, left his most explosive attackers, Leónidas and Tim, out of the semifinal lineup. He said he was saving them for the final. But Pimenta was planning a bit too far ahead, as goals by Gino Colaussi and Giuseppe Meazza within five minutes in the second half knocked Brazil out. Hungary, behind Gyula Zsengeller's hat trick, stormed past Sweden, 5–1, in the other semifinal.

The final, a matchup of Pozzo's strong and fast team, highly conditioned as always, against Hungary's elegant teamwork, produced a very attractive championship game. Pozzo withdrew his team to the sleepy Paris suburb of St. Germain to prepare for the June 19 showdown, and the tranquil respite worked. In the battle of the center forwards—Piola and Sarosi—the Italians won, 4–2. Colaussi and Pál Titkos traded early goals, but then Piola, Colaussi, and Piola again offset Sarosi's last gasp for Hungary.

Italy's direct and rapid attacks proved too much for the Magyars, who could not cope, despite their methodical tactics. Their era would come later. With the outbreak of world war, Italy retained the World Cup for 12 years, until the next FIFA tournament in 1950.

THE GOALSCORERS

Silvio Piola and Leónidas da Silva, the "Black Diamond," dominated the 1938 World Cup. This pair of center forwards accounted for 13 goals, Leónidas leading the count with 8 tallies.

Piola was Vittorio Pozzo's newest offensive weapon, the quintessential center forward until Gigi Riva came onto the Italian scene in the 1960s. He was big for his time (5 feet, 10 inches) and was built "like a rock," according to contemporary judgement. His career was spent primarily with Rome's Lazio club, with whom he twice led Italy in scoring. In the national team, he replaced Angelo Schiavio, scored 30 times, and played his last match at the age of 39, in 1952.

Leónidas, chosen for the first time for Brazil's national team in 1932, was a product of the streets of Rio, where he learned his soccer. After time with several small clubs, Leónidas played with Vasco da Gama, Botafogo, and Flamengo. He led Flamengo to three Rio championships and won three scoring titles (including a 43-goal-year in 1940). After the World Cup, the swift Brazilian went to Argentina's Boca Juniors. He finished up with São Paulo, winning five more state titles with them.

Nicknamed "the man of rubber," for the way he endured opponents' physical attacks, Leónidas was said to play "with soccer's Bible in his arms." He retired in 1950 to become a popular Brazilian radio and television commentator.

HAVANA MEMORIES

Cuba's presence in 1938 marked the island nation's only appearance in the World Cup and its only high-visibility soccer experience. Baseball won the battle for Cuba's national pastime and since 1938 the country has entered only 5 of the 10 World Cups. However, Cuba's goalkeeper made news in 1938. Benito Carvajales, dropped from the starting team for the first round replay against Romania, called his own press conference on the eve of the match to proclaim: "We shall win the replay. . .we shall score twice, they will score only one. Adios, caballeros." He was precisely right. But in the quarterfinals, Sweden sobered Carvajales and his mates, 8–0.

1950

The world was slowly emerging from war, and by 1950 FIFA felt capable of reinstituting the World Cup. Held in Brazil, which built the fabulous 200,000-place Maracaña Stadium expressly for the purpose, the prize of the 1950 World Cup was the first official Jules Rimet Cup, named after FIFA's president and the founder of the tournament.

Uruguay returned, but Argentina stayed away again, and France, Hungary, and Czechoslovakia were all missing. A new entrant to the World Cup was England, which had settled various long-standing political differences with FIFA (mostly debates about professionalism, as England still adhered to the amateur code for Olympic soccer) in 1946 and was eligible for the first time. The 1950 tournament reverted to the group format of 1930, in which four group winners advanced to a final round. After several withdrawals, the Brazilian World Cup opened with just 13 teams, leaving Uruguay and Bolivia alone in Group 4, and only three teams in Group 3.

Brazil, perhaps overconfident in its role as home team, stumbled against Switzerland, 2–2, in the opening match. The São Paulo police were called in to extricate the team from a stadium surrounded by angry fans. The team found themselves facing a must-win against Yugoslavia to reach the final pool, but Ademir and Zizinho found the net and Brazil escaped a first-round disaster.

Italy, still shaken by the loss of many of its finest players in a 1949 airplane crash in Turin, in which the players of the Torino team had all been killed, and without Vittorio Pozzo at the helm, failed, 3–2, to Sweden. Thus, the defending World Cup holders, who were so haunted by Turin that they traveled by boat to Brazil, were out.

But the biggest story of the first round came on June 29 on a miserable field in Belo Horizonte. The score was so unbelievable that newspaper offices in Europe demanded confir-

mation from their reporters: USA 1, England 0. Joe Gaetjens, a Haitian, who most likely was not an American citizen at the time, scored the winning goal after 39 minutes in what has become one of soccer's most memorable results. The United States had played just nine games since 1934 and the possibility that this nation could defeat England, still considered de facto the world's preeminent power, was unthinkable. Indeed, the United States did not win another game and did not advance past this round. Three days later, Spain delivered the coup de grace to England's first World Cup excursion, 1–0, and the self-proclaimed guardians of the game, who had first exported it to South America, were out.

The finals, played in a four-team group, produced marveluoly exciting soccer, probably the best seen to date in a World Cup. With a continuous samba beat in the stadium, the 200,000 fans at the Maracaña witnessed 8 days of thrilling exploits. Uruguay dropped a point to Spain, while Brazil roared past Sweden and Spain, scoring 13 goals and giving up just 2. This set up a Brazil–Uruguay match to decide the title. Due to Uruguay's failure against Spain, Brazil could finally claim soccer's Holy Grail with just a tie.

Brazil prepared with complete concentration, their own cooks, and special vitamin drinks. The feast was set for celebration. Friaça opened the scoring at 47 minutes and Maracaña turned into bedlam. But Obdulio Varela, a Uruguayan legend, the "El Jefe" of the team, pushed forward from his defensive position 19 minutes later to create Juan Schiaffino's equalizing goal. Alcides Ghiggia remembers the moment of his winning goal six minutes from the end: "I was at an impossible angle, I thought. Barbosa was trying to prevent a cross, giving me just a bit of room. I closed my eyes, hit the ball with all my energy, and when I opened them, it was in the goal and we were world champions."

Brazil played the 1950 tournament with all the skill and effervescence that have become its trademark. But the team fell at the final turn. FIFA's president Jules Rimet recalled the game's last seconds: "With the result 1–1, I passed through the tunnels of the gigantic stands. . .to present the Brazilians with the trophy. . .when I reached the spot, there was a deathly silence in the stadium. Uruguay had just scored. . . suddenly there were no guards of honor, no national anthem, no speeches, no magnificent victory celebrations." ⚽

URUGUAY'S PELÉ

Juan Schiaffino is among Uruguay's fabled stars. He was nicknamed Pepe from birth and along with his brother Raúl he was an example of unparalleled soccer technique. He starred for Peñarol and was called to the "Celeste," Uruguay's national team, in 1945. Lanky, and pale, Schiaffino was noted for his deceptive qualities on attack, skills which helped lead his teams to three Uruguayan titles as well as to the World Cup. In addition to his goal in the 1950 final, he scored four goals in the opening round game against Bolivia, making him one of nine players to score four times in a World Cup match. He later played for A. C. Milan and Roma and for Italy in the 1958 World Cup. ⚽

Although soccer has evolved since Langenus got police protection and life insurance before agreeing to referee the first World Cup Final, referees are still widely criticized. FIFA holds a pre-tournament (as here in 1950) to eliminate inconsistencies.

(Gazzetta dello Sport)

THE SWISS LOCK

Switzerland came to the 1950 World Cup an unfancied team. But they blazed a trail for soccer when they unveiled their *verrou* formation. The word means "bolt" in French and it called essentially for five backs, one playing behind the other four in a "sweeper" position. This caused difficulty for Brazil, who struggled to a 2–2 tie with the Swiss. In years to come, the *verrou* became better known to the world as *catenaccio*, the Italian version employed by Helanio Herrera in the 1960s. The defensive posture of teams using the formation became infamous as critics bemoaned the resulting lack of offensive flair and risk the game once encouraged. ⚽

With 38 entries, the 1954 tournament was the largest World Cup to date and finished as the highest scoring tournament ever. It was the era of European power teams, and especially of Hungary, the Magnificent Magyars, who came into the World Cup with a four-year undefeated streak. The Hungarians had emerged from behind the Iron Curtain to take the 1952 Olympic gold medal, to beat England at home—for that country's first ever home defeat after ninety years of soccer—and to set the standard for the sport throughout the decade. With Ferenc Puskás, Jószef Boszik, Sandor Kocsis, and Nandor Hidegkuti, among others, the team has been considered one of the finest of all time. But, as in 1950, the World Cup was to prove unpredictable. It was played in first round groups, with the winners and runners-up in each group proceeding directly to the knockout quarterfinals. In Group 1, Brazil again faced Yugoslavia (as they had in 1950) in the pivotal match and a 1–1 tie ensured that both went forward. Hungary easily advanced with incredible 9–0 and 8–3 wins over South Korea, the first Asian team to reach the World Cup finals, and West Germany, respectively.

Defending champion Uruguay turned back the Czechs in the Berne mud to reach the quarterfinals, alongside Austria from Group 3. From Group 4, an aging England team somewhat atoned for 1950's collapse by advancing with Switzerland.

The quarterfinals saw goals galore and the Battle of Berne, one of soccer's most sordid episodes. Tabbed as outsiders at best, West Germany stopped Yugoslavia, 2–0, to grab one semifinal spot, and Uruguay, though badly hobbled by injury, heroically turned aside England, 4–2. The other two matches live on, although for quite different reasons. Austria and Switzerland, playing in Lausanne, engaged in one of soccer's greatest games, Austria finally prevailing, 7–5.

Spelling the end of the unbeatable Magyars, Germany's Max Morlock scores the victorious team's first goal against Gyula Grosics in the 1954 final. Midfield master, Hungary's captain Ferenc Puskás (no. 9) watches the magic disappear.
(Farabolafoto)

It was Switzerland 3–0 after just seventeen minutes, but Austria exploded for three in three minutes from Alfred Körner, and Theodor Wagner (two goals). Körner and Ernst Ocwirk added two more before halftime and it was clear that Austria would carry the day.

Hungary and Brazil met in Berne under heavy rain and muddy conditions. When the game ended, Hungary had won, 4–2, but the real story was the four cautions, three expulsions, and two penalty kicks that marred the matchup of Europe and South America's finest sides. The gratuitous physical conduct of the Brazilians was chiefly blamed for the nature of the match, though neither side could claim innocence. With 18 minutes left, Boszik and Nilton Santos came to blows on the field and were sent off; but after the game the Brazilians continued the abysmal affair by invading the Hungarian locker-room. Finally police and sensible heads restored order.

The semifinals had no such drama, as Hungary put out Uruguay through goals by Zoltan Czibor, Hidegkuti, and a pair of overtime headers from Kocsis, and West Germany caused Austria's collapse. Fritz Walter, West Germany's titan of a center forward, scored twice to end Austrian hopes.

For the third straight World Cup, an attractive and heavily favored team reached the final, where an upstart would thwart them. Hungary had beaten West Germany, 8–3, in the opening round, and even with Puskás only partially healthy,

Hungary clearly was the critics' choice. West Germany's coach, Sepp Herberger, prepared his team for the final without making any reference to the first round game. What was past was past for Herberger.

Hungary quickly led 2–0 behind Puskás at six minutes and Czibor at eight, and it seemed that the Magyars would claim the prize they deserved. However, Germany responded through Maximilian Morlock at 10 minutes and Helmut Rahn at 18 minutes to destroy Hungary's momentum. Just six minutes from the end, Rahn's magnificent shot from a hard angle beat Grosics and West Germany took the cup.

For West Germany, the tournament was the first of many visits to the final; for Hungary, soon to be engulfed in revolution, it was the end of first-class international soccer; and for Brazil it was to be a watershed for their training methods. In 1950 the Brazilians had perhaps been too "individual," so for 1954 the coaches imposed an authoritarian approach. It, too, failed, but their soccer authorities had learned their lessons, and the world would be their pupils four years later in Sweden. ⚽

DANUBE MASTERS

Fritz Walter was a towering figure for West Germany, the first true "Kaiser" of Teutonic soccer. Blessed with great vision of the field and "sublime technical skill," Walter came from Kaiserslautern to the West German national team in 1940. His strong physical presence and cool psychological leadership was integral to West Germany's success in soccer after World War II.

Although he did not win a World Cup, Hungary's Ferenc Puskás is among soccer's all-time legends. He is one of the rare individuals who played for two different countries, representing Spain in 1962. The "Galloping Major," as he was quaintly nicknamed for his army rank, played 84 times for Hungary before defecting. He then gained further fame for his role with Real Madrid during the Spanish team's glory years in the 1960s. ⚽

THE MAGIC MAGYARS

Hungary developed into the superteam of the 1950s for several reasons. First, the nation had unusual talent in Puskás, Kocsis, Hidegkuti, Czibor, and Grosics. Second, the Iron Curtain countries' sports method of allocating the best talent to one team put most of the players in uniform and on the army team Honved. Great emphasis was put on training, which was nearly endless, and on strong moral fiber. Suspensions and public confession of wrongdoing were common. Their tactics were a variation on the 4–2–4 system (known as the WM formation, an interlocking midfield developed first in the 1930s), which Brazil would perfect in 1958, but primarily it was the overwhelming pool of talent that made Hungary nearly invincible. ⚽

1958

As 1954 was remembered as Hungary's World Cup, the 1958 version has always been known as Pelé's. Despite a somewhat undistinguished competition overall, the 1958 World Cup marked the emergence of the then 17-year old Brazilian who would carry the entire soccer world to new heights over his 20-year career.

Held in Sweden, the 1958 tournament was now fully mature, attracting 58 entries, and the prize was sought after by every major soccer-playing nation. After the disappointments of 1950 and 1954, Brazil finally displayed to the world that it could channel its bubbly individuality into a winning team format. Coach Vicente Feola, a short, rotund man, installed the 4–2–4 system, and had the perfect players to execute it. Pelé, Garrincha, and Mario Zagallo on the front line brought a completely new dimension of speed and spontaneity to attacking soccer and gave the first demonstration of the "South American" style, versus the more cerebral and physical "European" style of soccer, establishing stereotypes that were held for thirty years.

Played again in groups, the tournament produced a highly competitive first round, Northern Ireland, Wales, and the USSR, making its first World Cup appearance, were forced to playoffs before advancing to the quarterfinals alongside France, Sweden, West Germany, Yugoslavia, and Brazil. Brazil samba'd to the quarterfinals by beating Austria, tying England, and beating the USSR and the famed goalkeeper Lev Yachine. Pelé first took the field against the Soviets and contributed significantly as teammate Vavá scored twice. France provided the biggest first-round thrills, though, as Just Fontaine tallied six goals in wins over Paraguay and Scotland and a draw with Yugoslavia.

The expected form held up in the quarterfinals as Just Fontaine scored two more goals in France's win against Northern Ireland. Sweden, led by Kurt Hamrin, turned back the USSR. West Germany, with a rough and hard tackling style, stopped Yugoslavia, 1–0, but Brazil struggled against Wales, 1–0. Only Pelé's 66th-minute goal, from a shot that deflected off defender Stuart Williams' foot, made the difference.

The semifinals saw Pelé at his best, scoring a hat trick to eliminate the French, 5-2; Fontaine left with the highest scoring total of any player in the finals, 13 goals (the closest are Kocsis with 11 goals in 1954 and Gerd Müller with 10 in 1970) but without a medal. Sweden, with an energetic and vocal home crowd, used the leadership of veterans Nils Liedholm and Gunnar Gren to sweep the defending-champion West Germans out of the tournament. Lennart Skoglund, Gren, and Hamrin scored in the Swede's 3–1 win, which gave Scandinavian soccer its only appearance in a World Cup Final.

In the final, Brazil was as heavily favored as they had been in 1950 and as the Hungarians had been in 1954. This time, there would be no upset. With their great flair overwhelming Sweden's older, slower team, Brazil dominated throughout. Garrincha, with his remarkable acceleration, twice split Sweden's defense to set up Vavá at 10 and 32 minutes, after

At seventeen, Pelé won the world's heart when Brazil's 1958 conquest brought him inconsolable tears of joy. Retiring at Giants Stadium, in 1977, he asked spectators to recite his motto that soccer was above all about "love, love, love."
(Farabola)

host team did not flaunt its national colors before the opponent. Not only did he wave the flag, he asked the crowd to follow his lead in cheering. They responded mightily with patriotic songs and chanting. Officials of the West German federation were not amused, appealed to FIFA, and were rewarded when the international body banned all "organized cheerleading" at the Sweden–Brazil championship match four days later. ⚽

Liedholm had given the Swedes false hope just three minutes into the game. At the end it was an emphatic 5–2 for Brazil, the first and only team to win the World Cup outside their home hemisphere. One commentator wrote, "We saw football which was just out of this world." And this world was to see much more of it four years later. ⚽

THE ONE PELÉ

When Pelé took the field on June 15, 1958, against the USSR, he was the youngest player ever to compete in a World Cup. When he finally retired from the World Cup's fields twelve years later, he was (and still is) the only man to be on a team to win three World Cup titles.

Named Edson Arantes do Nascimento, Pelé (using a single name, as many Brazilian players have chosen to do) was the dominant man in soccer throughout his career, leading his club, Santos, to two World Club Championships, 11 São Paulo League titles, and he won the Paulista scoring title 11 times (his career tally was 1284 goals). One of the few recipients of FIFA's Order of Merit, Pelé came to the U.S. to end his career with the New York Cosmos, who won the league title in his final game in 1977. He played 117 times for Brazil, scoring 95 times and earning the straightforward nickname "O Rei," "The King." ⚽

CROWD CONTROL

Modern sports fans, who are accustomed to giant television replay screens in stadiums and team mascots who exhort the crowd, let alone soccer crowds who create their own organized pandemonium, would be amused by the so-called breach of sportsmanship at the 1958 World Cup. At the Gothenburg semifinal, between Sweden and West Germany, the Swedes engaged in some unbridled chauvinism that left a bad taste in some more conservative mouths.

A Swedish father figure, dressed in a neat blue blazer and carrying the Swedish flag, marched onto the field prior to the game, breaking all prior protocol, which held that the

1962

Chile, a nation perennially on the periphery of international soccer power, had been awarded the 1962 World Cup. Earthquakes devastated the nation in 1960 and Chilean president Carlos Dittborn exhorted FIFA to give Chile the tournament, "because we have nothing."

In the end, the tournament was an unattractive competition, marked by the lowest scoring output (2.78 goals per game) that had been seen since the World Cup's inception in 1930. But it was certainly won by the best team. Brazil, even without Pelé, who was injured in the second game, stood atop all the others. Coach Aymore Moreira had brought Amarildo of Botafogo into the squad, increased Garrincha's role, and asked even more than the usual from the versatile Mario Zagallo. It all worked.

Brazil easily went through the first round group to the quarterfinals. Pelé scored a memorable goal, dribbling past five Mexican defenders in the opening game, but it was to be his last goal and last full game of this World Cup. In the second match, against Czechoslovakia, "O Rei" pulled a left thigh muscle while hitting the post with a rocket shot after 25 minutes. He limped from the field, out of the World Cup, which suffered for his absence.

Elsewhere in the first round, West Germany and Chile were victors, while the rebuilt Hungary, led by Florian Albert, and England, with such young players as Jimmy Greaves, Bobby Moore, and Bobby Charlton, made it past the first round for only the second time in four tries. The USSR and Yugoslavia were easy winners in their group.

The quarterfinal knockout round produced little drama, but confirmed Brazil's role as overwhelming favorite. The Brazilians gave England a lesson in South American style with a 3–1 win at Viña del Mar. Garrincha scored twice, one on a header and another off Vavá's free kick. Vavá himself got the third, while Reg Hitchens' 38th-minute goal was all England could muster. It would be another World Cup before England could enjoy victory.

Chile, in front of an extremely vociferous home audience in

Arica, turned back the USSR on goals by Leonel Sanchez and Eladio Rojas. The Soviets openly blamed Lev Yachine, their world-class goalie, for both Chilean goals, and went home beaten, to ponder why their recent Olympic and European Championship titles did not translate into World Cup success. Yugoslavia gained revenge over West Germany, meeting them for the third straight tournament in the quarterfinals and finally winning, 1–0, via Petar Radakovic's goal. Czechoslovakia quietly eliminated Hungary in the other match.

In a trademark cartwheel move, Brazil's Garrincha (foot and hand barely visible) surprises players in the 4–2 1962 semifinal between Brazil and Chile.
(Farabolafoto)

Chile's dream ended abruptly at the feet of Garrincha and his teammates in the semifinals. Garrincha could not be contained and scored twice while setting up Vavá for a third in Brazil's 4–2 win. It was rumored that Brazil's president listened to the match on headphones while attending mass, such was the interest in the team's progress. Czechoslovakia unremarkably defeated the Yugoslavs, 3–1, to claim its second appearance in the final and to form the second straight European–South American championship game.

Some of the glamor was missing in the final due to Pelé's injury. But Brazil thoroughly dominated Czechoslovakia, 3–1, behind goals by Amarildo, Zito, and Vavá. Due to Pelé's unavailability, Coach Moreira was forced to use Zagallo in a deeper-lying role rather than up front. This resulted in the creation of a 4–3–3 formation with only one true winger. Only Zagallo's incredible stamina and athletic ability allowed such a switch to be made, but it was another demonstration of how powerful the Brazilians were in the late 1950s and early 1960s. ⚽

BRAZIL'S ICARUS

Garrincha, whose full name was Manoel dos Santos Francisco, was the seventh son of a nightwatchman. He always dreamed of becoming a soccer star, and his fluid, speedy moves as a youngster earned him the nickname "Garrincha," Little Bird. He joined Botafogo as a young teenager and quickly became famous for his explosive attacking runs and for his passing. The World Cup finals of 1958 and 1962 earned him a place among soccer's all-time greats, but perhaps unable to handle the fame, Garrincha lost his desire to play and allowed himself to disintegrate physically. The all-time No. 1 right winger died in 1983, broke and broken. ⚽

FOREVER ZAGALLO

Unheralded but perhaps the key to Brazil's second straight World Cup was Mario Zagallo. He came to Brazil's national team just a month prior to the 1958 World Cup due and only due to an unfortunate injury to another player. But Zagallo brought enormous tactical savvy to the team, playing on the front line in the famous 4–2–4 formation. It was his tireless runs that set up so much Pelé and Vavá magic. Retiring to the coach's bench in 1966, Zagallo coached Brazil to the 1970 World Cup title, was assistant coach in 1994, and head coach again in 1998, returning Brazil to its stylish attacking roots. In 1990 he coached the United Arab Emirates in the World Cup finals. ⚽

1966

By the mid-1960s the World Cup was a global affair, with television beginning to broadcast the tournament to the remotest corners of the world. But the 1966 edition also marked a temporary end to the enchanting soccer practiced by the Brazilians and the substitution of a hard, high work-rate style. Some individual brilliance did exist, to be sure, but generally the 1966 tournament, played in England, did not achieve high levels of creative play until the semifinals.

Pelé was hurt again, this time by a despicable foul, and out of the competition early on. Without him, Brazil was a shadow of itself and never was a factor. The tournament story revolved more around England.

When Alf Ramsey took over as England coach in 1962, he bluntly forecast, "England will win the World Cup." Sticking to his pet theory that specialty players no longer made sense and that work rate was the key factor to soccer success, the undiplomatic and taciturn Ramsey shaped a team to fulfill his promise. He called his players "the wingless wonders," using a formation that influenced the next soccer era to a great extent. (Although it worked for England, it contributed to the general decline of attractive European soccer in the late 1960s and early 1970s).

England, though not impressive at all, made it through the first round, alongside Uruguay, West Germany, Argentina, Portugal, and Hungary. They key story of the round was the brutal treatment of Pelé and Brazil's elimination. Pelé had been marked tightly in the opening game against Bulgaria and could not compete in Brazil's second match, against Hungary, a 3–1 loss. Returning against Portugal, Pelé was viciously fouled by Morais and was carried from the field. Brazil exited the tournament, losing 3–1.

The Soviet Union and mysterious North Korea also survived. The North Koreans, behind a nearly impenetrable language barrier, were totally unknown, though it was learned that they were mostly military personnel. They ultimately left an indelible mark on the World Cup, however, knocking heavily favored Italy out of the competition, 1–0. Pak Doo-Ik, later the North Korea head coach, scored in the 41st minute to send the Italians packing. The Azzurri returned to Italian soil ignominiously—and famously, to a torrent of rotten tomatoes hurled by angry fans who met them at the airport.

The tournament came to life at last in the quarterfinals. England and Argentina played a bitter match at Wembley, where Geoff Hurst's header after 77 minutes made the dif-ference. But the lingering memory of the match was the expulsion of Argentina's Antonio Rattin. His overzealous dispute following referee Kreitlein's warning to a teammate led to a red-card confrontation, Rattin's subsequent provocative refusal to leave the field, and Ramsey's post-game utterance that the Argentine players were "animals." Twenty years later that remark still was alive in Argentine minds and would figure in another World Cup quarterfinal showdown. West Germany, Portugal—with the Mozambique-born Eusebio, Africa's first international soccer star, scoring 4 goals against North Korea—and the USSR also reached the semifinals.

West Germany stopped the Soviets, 2–1, at Liverpool, and for the second straight World Cup tournament the great Lev Yachine was blamed for both the goals which knocked Russia out. England and Portugal engaged in a dazzling semifinal game at Wembley, won by England, 2–1. Nobby Stiles snuffed out Eusebio's offense and Bobby Charlton scored twice to complement Gordon Banks' brilliant late save from Coluna. Thus England and West Germany, deepest historic rivals, were set for the final.

Televised around the world, the 1966 World Cup final had technical brilliance and high drama. But Hurst, from West Ham United, stole the show with the first hat trick in a World Cup Final. Through goals by Hurst and his club teammate Martin Peters,

On a breakaway in the very last seconds of extra time, as fans were already invading the pitch in celebration, Geoff Hurst scored a breathtaking solo goal, his third of the match, to seal the 1966 World Cup for England.

(Olympia)

ENGLAND 3 GERMANY W. 2

England led as time evaporated for the Germans. One last lunge in injury time, with fifteen seconds left, rescued West Germany, when Wolfgang Weber scored off a pass from Siggi Held.

During the interval before the start of extra time, Ramsey gathered his team with the counsel, "Well, you won it once; you'll just have to win it again." And they did, behind two more Hurst goals. The first struck the underside of the bar and came down over (or did it?) the line. The enduring controversy about whether the goal was legal is still alive, but quite irrelevant since the Swiss referee, after conferring with his linesman, validated the score. A few seconds before the game ended, Hurst scored again on a counterattack. Captain Bobby Moore, whose club team was also West Ham, then accepted the World Cup from Queen Elizabeth II, and England was finally crowned the world's champion. ⚽

ENGLAND'S REDEEMER

At the end of the 1966 World Cup Final, defender Nobby Stiles ran up to Alf Ramsey and blurted out "You did it, Alf. We'd have been nothing without you." The quiet family man firmly believed in himself, his players and his methods, despite frequent attacks from fans and media. He was shy and shunned the limelight; yet underneath he was an aggressive man who insisted that his authority be respected by his players. He rebuilt the image of English soccer by finding an unusual blend of players who could carry out the work-oriented style he believed in. His players believed equally in the system and in themselves. Many observers criticized his player selections, but when the World Cup was firmly in England's hands, those critics were silenced, at least until the next tournament. ⚽

MAGIC SLIPPERS

Tiny, redheaded Alan Ball typified the type of player Alf Ramsey wanted for his England team. Ball was key to his country's triumph, running endlessly. He recalled the extra-time period: "Now we had to win it again, as Alf said. We went into it in that frame of mind and ran them off their feet. Tiredness did not come into it. During those final minutes I could not hear the crowd or anything. Something was just driving me on and on." Perhaps it was the thought of climbing the famous 39 steps at Wembley to accept the Jules Rimet Cup. ⚽

1970

The oppressive midday heat and the altitude were two factors that influenced the 1970 World Cup, held in Mexico. Europeans frequently blame the climatic conditions for England's failure to keep possession of the World Cup, but a better analysis is that the 1970 tournament proved Brazil's brilliance at the expense of the negative, Italian *catenaccio* defensive system now employed by many of the European national teams.

Mexico was awarded the World Cup in 1964, during a meeting of soccer's world authorities. Numerous allegations were made that the votes were "bought" by political influence and it is a fact that no one inspected any Mexican facilities to see whether the nation was capable of hosting the event. Following the award, FIFA President Sir Stanley Rous put into place some regulations regarding World Cup sites, which are the forerunners of the modern practice of extensive inspection and written guarantees.

Once politics was out of the way and the games begun, it was clear that Brazil, England, West Germany, and Italy were the favorites. Brazil, which in typical emotional fashion had changed its head coach just two months before the competition, trained and conditioned very carefully for the heat and altitude that their site, Guadalajara, would require. England was defending its title, but the Alf Ramsey reference to Argentina's "animals" clung to the team and angered Mexican fans.

Brazil and England were grouped together in the opening round and with Pelé, Tostão, and Gerson in top form, the Brazilians swept past everyone. Jairzinho's 59th-minute goal toppled England, 1–0, in a matchup of the two previous World Cup winners.

The knockout quarterfinals provided an extraordinary West Germany–England matchup, a replay of the '66 final. England were winning, 2–0, with twenty minutes to go, but lost, 3–2, in overtime, and Ramsey was loudly criticized for complacently taking off playmaker Bobby Charlton in the second half, allegedly opening up spaces for the Germans' attack. However, German midfielder Jürgen Grabowski's heart and legs were the really decisive factors.

The semifinals produced an easy win by Brazil over Uruguay and a stunning 4–3 overtime victory by Italy over the weary Germans, who had yet to recover from the England game just three days earlier. Italy led, 1–0, as time dwindled, but Grabowski and Karl-Heinz Schnellinger combined to tie the game in the third minute of injury time. From then on, the scoring was fast and furious. Extra-time goals by Tarcisio Burgnich, Luigi Riva, and Gianni Rivera carried Italy to its third final. Franz Beckenbauer, Germany's libero and field general, played much of the game with a dislocated shoulder, and his reduced effectiveness may well have kept West Germany from its second straight final.

But Italian joy was shortlived. The matchup between Brazil's flashy offense and Italy's defensive shell was intriguing, but with Pelé leading the way, Brazil showed the world what beautiful, attacking soccer can be. Pelé scored once and set up two other goals as Brazil powered to a 4–1 victory. That three-goal margin is a World Cup Final record. By virtue of its third win, Brazil took permanent possession of the Jules Rimet Trophy, retiring it from competition, to be replaced by the FIFA World Cup Trophy. ⚽

SAMBA SOCCER

Brazil in 1970 was the embodiment of exciting, expressive soccer. No team since has produced such a vibrant style of play, nor has any captivated the world as Brazil did then. Indeed, thereafter Brazil has been the team the world universally cheers for during the World Cup.

Pelé, Roberto Rivelino, Tostão, Clodoaldo, Gerson, Felix, Jairzinho, Carlos Alberto, Wilson Piazza, Everaldo, and Brito were the eleven who lined up for the 1970 World Cup Final and all have become household names. Certainly Pelé gave the team its character, because of his scoring ability, his vision on the field, and his uncanny passing. Only a 17-year-old in Sweden in 1958 and personally disappointed in 1962 and 1966, Pelé used the 1970 World Cup to prove his place in soccer history. Tostão's speed and twisting runs, Rivelino's rocket-like free kicks, Clodoaldo's playmaking skills, and Jairzinho's blinding speed have all become part of soccer lore and together gave the 1970 World Cup an élan quite unique. ⚽

SAVING HISTORY

The most memorable save in history? It probably came in the match between England and Brazil in 1970. Jairzinho started an attack with incredible acceleration. He swept to the endline and centered to the far post, where Pelé rose and headed the ball down. He was already whirling away, arms punching the air, and shouting to celebrate "goal," as Gordon Banks somehow lunged backwards across the goalmouth to push the ball over the bar. "He came up like a salmon out of fresh water," said the astounded Pelé. "At that moment I hated him more than any man in soccer. When I cooled down, I had to applaud him with my heart." English writer John Moynihan described "an outrageous flash of movement. . .his colleagues too nonplussed to yell their praise. Already the moment had become a legend, a piece of unique folklore. . . ." ⚽

Teeming with virtuosos, Brazil retired the Jules Rimet Trophy in 1970. The team won so overwhelmingly that Pelé (holding the trophy) claimed the next morning he had to call his wife to be sure the game hadn't been a dream.

(Olympia)

54

1974

Brazil's victories in the 1970 World Cup and on various world tours had encouraged many teams to "go Brazilian" and play adventurously. The West Germans and the Dutch took the lesson to heart and brought a very high level of tactics and skill to the 1974 World Cup, which for the first time was held in West Germany.

The Germans had been entrusted with the World Cup in 1964 and had a full decade to prepare for it. As a result, the Germans produced a wonderful tournament, despite the grey and rainy conditions which prevailed for most of the 24-day event. In the end, it came down to a duel between the two pre-eminent teams in Europe, West Germany and the Netherlands. The Dutch were proponents of what head coach Rinus Michels called "Total Football," in which all 11 men played offense or defense, depending upon ball possession. Perhaps this wasn't as original a concept as the Dutch claimed, but with Johan Cruyff—Holland's superlative playmaker and goal scorer—Johan Neeskens, and Johnny Rep up front and Ruud Krol and Wim Suurbier on the back line, Holland's 1974 team was as good as any ever produced in Europe.

West Germany had less flair, but Gerd Müller, a prolific goalscorer known as "Der Bomber," and Franz Beckenbauer anchored a remarkable team that arguably was the most consistent team in the 1970s.

The first round produced East Germany's 1–0 win over West Germany—a temporary shock. The Dutch reminded viewers of the talented Hungarians of 1954, and the Poles, with Wladislaw Zmuda and Gregorz Lato, emerged as a contender. Under the unusual organization of the tournament, first round victors were grouped into two second round pools rather than advancing to a knockout phase. In Group A, Holland kept its undefeated streak alive, humbling Argentina, 4–0, East Germany, 2–0, and Brazil, the defending champion, 2–0. Dutch Total Football seemed to all comers completely unbeatable. In Group B, West Germany too went undefeated, finally turning back Poland, 1–0, on Gerd Müller's 75th-minute goal in the decisive match of the second round.

In the Olympic Stadium in Munich, before 77,833 fans, West Germany and the Netherlands took

Tripped, before even touching the ball, in the first minute of the 1974 final, Johan Cruyff scored from the resulting penalty, but Holland still stumbled, losing to West Germany, 2–1.

(Popperfoto)

the field for the final. Prince Bernhard of the Netherlands greeted his team; West German President Walter Scheel exhorted his team; United States Secretary of State Henry Kissinger was among the fans.

The Dutch opened quickly. Cruyff was tripped in the penalty area by Uli Hoeness before West Germany had even touched the ball, and Neeskens calmly converted the penalty—the first in the final's history—in the first minute. But as Brazil in 1950, Hungary in 1954, Sweden in 1958, Czechoslovakia in 1962, and West Germany in 1966 could attest, the team which scores first doesn't necessarily win.

For the Dutch this quickly came true. Paul Breitner equalized on a penalty at 25 minutes after Wim Jansen had tripped Bernd Hölzenbein in another overzealous bit of defense. At this point Holland lost its rhythm, and Müller shot cleanly through Krol's legs in the 43rd minute to give West Germany victory, 2–1. Berti Vogts, Germany's coach since the 1990 World Cup, shadowed Cruyff throughout the afternoon, despite giving several inches away to him in height, and effectively eliminated Holland's greatest weapon from the game. Helmut Schoen's West Germans had the second World Cup in the nation's history. ⚽

FORWARD AND BACK

Johan Cruyff and Franz Beckenbauer, soccer's guiding lights of the 1970s, were opposites in personality. Cruyff was known as the "enfant terrible" of European soccer, while Beckenbauer was always noted for his gentlemanly approach to opponents and fans.

Cruyff led his club Ajax Amsterdam and Dutch soccer in general out of the shadows with his stunning ability. With the ball at his foot, no one, perhaps not even Pelé, could match the lithe Cruyff for ability. Always outspoken and surrounded by controversial, equally outspoken advisers and family members, Cruyff was playing with Barcelona by the time of the 1974 World Cup and later played for many different teams. The traditional pattern was for Cruyff and the team coach to disagree, sometimes resulting in the coach being fired and sometimes with Cruyff picking up and moving on. Despite his strong-willed manner, his rare imagination on the field remains a perfect illustration of what soccer can be all about. Only Cruyff could reinvent the penalty kick, once bemusing a stadium by eschewing the direct shot and instead passing sideways to a teammate, who passed the ball back for Cruyff to chip over the fallen goalkeeper. "You only have to make sure the referee is capable of following this," he later said mischievously.

Beckenbauer revolutionized the game from his defensive position. He played as a young man in the 1966 World Cup Final but received little notice. By 1974, he had changed the game's tactics, having developed the role of libero in his own image; the libero became an offensive defender, bringing the ball forward, into the attack. The concept of such a talented defender moving forward directing the attack con-

founded opponents and helped break down the strict *catenaccio* thinking prevalent at the start of the 1970s. Primarily a star with Bayern Munich, whom he led to three European Cups, Beckenbauer briefly joined the New York Cosmos of the N.A.S.L., ultimately became head coach of Germany, and coached his unified nation to victory in the 1990 World Cup Final. ⚽

TOTAL SYMMETRY

In the early 1970s, the European balance of soccer power was clear: Ajax Amsterdam of Holland had won three straight European Cups, followed immediately by a Bayern Munich triple. The national teams mirrored these two clubs. Five of Holland's starters were from Ajax Amsterdam (Cruyff was with Barcelona in 1974, but his background was 100 percent Ajax). Six from Bayern Munich lined up for the final, including Beckenbauer and Müller. ⚽

1978

The 1978 World Cup in Argentina was the last 16-team tournament and among the most colorful and emotional of all time. The brilliance of Argentina's Mario Kempes, the second near miss by the Dutch, and the first glimpse of Michel Platini's elegant French team were highlights that stir memories in soccer fans worldwide.

The unusual tournament format, a repeat of 1974, also provided some memorable incidents, not all of them positive. The organization called for six first round pools of teams and two second round pools, from which the semifinalists would emerge. However, the fact that kickoff times were not simultaneous within groups allowed some teams the advantage of knowing exactly the task ahead of them prior to taking the field. Some irregularities occurred.

Brazil was heavily rebuilt after the collapse of 1974, and Holland was without Johan Cruyff, who had retired from international soccer. Most of the other Dutch stars returned under new head coach Ernst Happel for another try at soccer's top prize.

In the first round, Italy and Argentina were drawn into the same group, with Italy winning the head-to-head confrontation, 1–0, on Roberto Bettega's 67th-minute goal. Both advanced, however. Poland and West Germany came out of their group, though West Germany tripped against Tunisia, 0–0, and Poland won the group. Brazil, too, had its difficulties, barely scraping out a 1–0 win over Austria in a must-win situation for the three-time World Cup winners. The Brazilian fans' disillusionment put even greater pressure on Zico, Dirceu, Rivelino, and his teammates. Peru and the Netherlands also advanced.

The Netherlands was in top form and growing stronger game by game as the second round began. Happel's team

Riding a thundering wave of Argentine nationalism in a stadium wrapped in blue streamers and on a field covered in a sea of confetti, Mario Kempes almost inexorably broke the Dutch opposition to secure the 1978 World Cup.

(Olympia)

he gave to Italy in the 19th minute) and Arie Haan.

Controversy continues to swirl around Group B and Argentina's performance against Peru in the final match. Brazil had won earlier in the day against Poland and held a two-point lead and a goal difference of plus-five in the standings. Argentina faced the seemingly impossible task of beating Peru by four goals or Brazil would play for the World Cup. There has never been substantiation of any Peruvian complicity, but Argentina scored early and often against Ramón Quiroga, and a 6–0 Argentine victory went into the books. Kempes and Leopoldo Luque had two goals each, while René Houseman and Alberto Tarantini each scored once in one of soccer's most factious results.

The final was a thriller. The crowd in Buenos Aires' River Plate Stadium was a twelfth man for Argentina, erupting with a memorable cascade of blue and white confetti at the team's entrance. The game really matched the entire Argentine nation against the Dutch eleven and the president of the country declared prior to the game that "it is through the courage of all our people that we have reached the final." Players publicly prayed for victory and promised their countrymen they would not fail. In the face of such nationalism,

seemed destined this time, sweeping aside Austria, 5–1, tying West Germany, 2–2, and then beating Italy, 2–1, in the decisive match of Group A. The game against Italy was among the finest ever played by Holland and featured brilliant goals by Erny Brandts (making up for an own-goal

Argentina put an end to Holland's Total Football team, 3–1, though it took extra-time to win the World Cup.

The ever-present Kempes scored at 38 and 105 minutes, while Daniel Bertoni added an insurance goal six minutes from the end. Dirk Nanninga, a little known Dutch player, had brought Holland even in the 81st minute and it even seemed the Orangemen might change the game's momentum. But when Rob Rensenbrink smashed a ball off the left post in the final minute of regulation time, the Dutch efforts died. ⚽

PRODIGAL SON

Mario Alberto Kempes was the overwhelming star of the 1978 World Cup, leading the tournament in scoring and supplying the winning goal in the final. Although he never again attained such acclaim for his soccer, his long hair and effusive post-goal celebrations made him easily recognizable to fans everywhere. He came to Argentina's national team amid controversy; many Argentines felt that head coach César Menotti should not reach out to an Argentine playing in a foreign country, as Kempes had left Argentina to play for more money in Spain with Valencia. They felt that there were enough players still within Argentina's borders to avoid recruiting a "traitor" like Kempes. They were proven wrong and in the end Menotti's choice gave the World Cup many bright moments. Kempes first came to prominence in 1972 with Cordoba and then moved to Rosario Central, where he scored 25 goals in his first season. He was called to the national team in 1973 and was signed by Valencia in 1974 for $600,000. His career subsequently took him to various Spanish and Austrian clubs. ⚽

UP IN ARMS

Unfortunately an event such as the World Cup finals frequently becomes embroiled in politics. The 1978 competition was an example. No one doubted Argentina's soccer credentials to host the tournament, but with three years to go nothing was ready. No stadiums had been built or renovated and there was a call to move the tournament to neighboring Brazil. There was also resistance to allowing the military government of General Videla such a high-visibility event. FIFA, however, stepped in on March 24, 1976, declaring firmly that Argentina would remain the site. Argentina responded to the vote of confidence by issuing a military decree that effectively allowed the government to undertake directly whatever was necessary. By 1978, all was ready. ⚽

One of FIFA President João Havelange's primary goals when he was elected in 1974 was to increase the number of participants in the World Cup finals, opening it up to more soccer nations. The 1982 edition in Spain was the first of the 24-team tournaments. FIFA faced a great deal of criticism as soccer purists worried about a drop in quality of play, and the first round matches added fuel to this argument. But by the time the heat of competition and of early summer in Spain had intensified, the World Cup became remembered for two very special players: Michel Platini of France, a very stylish player with great perception for incisive passes, and Paolo Rossi of Italy, an infectious goal scorer whose two-year-long ban for alleged game fixing was ended just before the finals. Both played their best club football for Juventus in Turin.

The first round featured 32 games and 5 World Cup debutantes—Cameroon, Algeria, Honduras, Kuwait, and New Zealand. As expected, the newcomers did not advance, but Algeria provided one earthshaking result, toppling West Germany, 2–1. Neighbors West Germany and Austria were also involved in a memorable result, when the Germans won the decisive Group 2 match, 1–0, a suspicious score which eliminated Algeria and allowed the fraternal Germans and Austrians to advance. Great choruses of "fix" were heard, but Algeria still went home.

The first round games generally produced very cautious soccer, with teams playing not to lose rather than committing themselves to winning, attacking styles. This inspired constructive remedies four years later.

The second round pools provided some thrilling games. Poland reached the semifinals for the second time in three World Cups and West Germany snuck through by barely beating Spain and tying England. England's disheartening 0–0 draw with Spain in their final match of the round gave Germany its semifinal passport.

Italy, after a dismal first round of negative soccer, moved up a notch, improving with every match and quickly became the focus of the tournament. The mechanics of the finals grouped Italy, Argentina, and Brazil together in the second round and the games were among the most exciting ever played in the World Cup. Italy, through goals by Marco Tardelli and Antonio Cabrini, dispatched Argentina, 2–1, to deliver a blow to Argentina's hopes of retaining the trophy. Brazil then ended the champions' hopes, 3–1, in a match that saw rising superstar Diego Maradona sent off, to his and to Argentina's disgrace.

Brazil's natural penchant for attacking, in a game they needed only to tie to advance, may have worked against them in their next match, against Italy, but it provided for a breathtaking game. Rossi opened for Italy at 5 minutes, medical doctor Socrates replied for Brazil 3 minutes later; Rossi again scored after 25 minutes, and Paulo Roberto Falcao, a star for Italian club Roma, brought Brazil level again at 68 minutes. Finally, Rossi put Italy into the semifinals, with his hat-trick goal at 74 minutes. Brazil were out, but they achieved worldwide admiration for attacking at all times, even when Italy's counterattack was threatening them.

Releasing the energy his team had harnessed to survive a critical press and the opposition of Cameroon, Argentina, Brazil, Poland, and West Germany, Tardelli wheels away after scoring Italy's second goal in the 3–1 final win.

(Olympia)

Italy now brimmed with confidence, easily pushing aside Poland in one semifinal, 2–0, behind two more Rossi goals. West Germany and France, however, played a classic in the other match. It was the first World Cup game ever decided by penalty kicks. Despite the French building a two-goal lead in overtime the Germans still pushed the game to penalties. The penalty phase went to the sixth round; when France's Maxime Bossis missed, Germany's Horst Hrubesch calmly scored for the 5–4 win. The final was an anticlimax, though a quality match. Both teams played carefully, probing for an opponent's mistake; Rossi finally opened the floodgates and he, Tardelli, and Alessandro Altobelli gave Italy its third World Cup. ⚽

BRAVO ROSSI

World Cups seem to spawn a superstar, and in 1982 it was Paolo Rossi. The rail-thin Italian forward had suffered injuries and a match-fixing scandal when he arrived in Spain. Pablito's club success came primarily with Juventus of Turin (1972–75, 1981–85), where he was instrumental in helping the club to win three European trophies in addition to three Italian Championships and the Italian Cup. He played 48 times for Italy and capped the 1982 World Cup by being named European Footballer of the Year. Though always feared as an attacker, Rossi seemed to transcend even his reputation in the '82 World Cup. ⚽

PENALTY KICKS

The heat was stifling in Seville's Estadio Sánchez Pizjuan as France and West Germany struggled through 120 minutes of play and faced the first penalty-kick decision in World Cup history. The players were beyond exhaustion when referee Corver of the Netherlands finally blew his whistle. The French, captivating followers with their flair, had the game won with 22 minutes to play in extra time. Surely France would earn its deserved spot in the final. But Karl-Heinz Rummenigge and Klaus Fischer replied for West Germany in 10 furious minutes.

The drama was intense as the two very talented teams lined up to decide the match. Through the first three rounds of penalties, no one missed. Then Uli Stielike of West Germany had his shot saved by Jean-Luc Ettori to give France an opening. But Didier Six returned the favor, shooting directly at Harald Schumacher. No one else faltered until the sixth round, when veteran Maxime Bossis' shot along the ground was taken easily by the West German 'keeper. Horst Hrubesch then stepped up, fired to Ettori's left while the French goalie dove to his right, and it was over. The final score was 5–4 in penalties, after a 3-all draw. ⚽

1986

Diego Maradona of Argentina stole the World Cup headlines in 1986. But just getting the world to Mexico was a story of its own. Originally the 1986 tournament had been awarded to Colombia, but when the finals were expanded to 24 teams and subsequent domestic financial crises arose, the South American nation was forced to renounce its claim.

Two of the world's greatest playmakers in the 1980s and 1990s: Argentina's Diego Maradona is closely matched by Germany's Lothar Matthäus in the 1986 final. They met again in the 1990 final.

(Olympia)

Thus, with just three years to go, FIFA had no site for its jewel. The international body awarded Mexico its second host role, causing outcries that FIFA had ignored better qualified candidates (notably the United States). Plus, the European factions revived the heat and altitude arguments which haunted the 1970 games. But Mexico it was, and not even a devastating earthquake nine months before kickoff could knock Mexico off track.

In response to the dullness of play in Spain, the format was altered, allowing 16 teams to advance from six first round groups. The tournament had a knockout format from the eighth-finals onwards. The result was dramatic, yielding two thrilling quarterfinals, but also some dismay over the controversial penalty-kick system.

The form chart held up through the first round and through the eighth-finals, where Belgium and the USSR played to an incredible 4–3 overtime game. For the third straight World Cup, West Germany had a problem against an African qualifier, barely escaping Morocco, 1–0, through a Lothar Matthäus free kick.

The quarterfinals brought spine-tingling drama; three of the four games were decided by penalty kicks, including a Brazil–France match, that has been called one of the greatest games ever played. Tied 1–1 after overtime, the French finally prevailed 4–3 on penalties to give Michel Platini one last shot at a World Cup. Off form though (he even missed his penalty shootout kick), and growing old along with several of his teammates, Platini would have to look back at the game against Brazil as his last great moment. The world also focused on another quarter-final: England vs. Argentina. It was the first match between the two since the bitter Falklands War and it was seen by many as a morality play. Latin Americans had still not forgotten Alf Ramsey's "animals" remark of 1966, either. Diego Maradona saw it, however, as a chance to put his stamp on the World Cup forever. The stocky "little man" scored both goals in Argentina's 2–0 victory in extraordinary fashion, one quite illegally punched in with his hand ("It was the hand of God," Maradona categorically explained afterwards), which the referee nevertheless allowed, and one just minutes later with a 40-yard slalom-like run that was unstoppable. He darted through the entire England defense and finally deceived goalkeeper Peter Shilton to score one of the finest goals in World Cup history.

With emotions drained at the quarterfinal round, the semis merely confirmed the obvious: Argentina shut out Belgium, 2–0, on two Maradona goals, and the Germans again ousted the fading French by the same score. In the final, which was West Germany's fourth in the past six World Cups, Argentina and Maradona took their deserved prize. The Germans, high achievers without flamboyance, rallied heroically from a 2–0 deficit to draw even with both goals late in the second half, after Rummenigge and Völler took charge of the German offense. But Maradona, with uncanny instincts for the coun-

terattack, sent Jorge Burruchaga away for the winner in the 83rd minute. "A goal," a commentator wrote, "so unusual, almost romantic that it might have been scored by some schoolboy hero." "It was Diego's personal adventure," said teammate Valdano.

DOUBLE DANGER

As Pelé dominated the 1958 World Cup and Johan Cruyff symbolized the '74 tournament, Diego Armando Maradona, only five feet six inches but of hot temper and high skills, was the story of 1986. Left out of the 1978 Argentine team by César Menotti, who took great public heat for the decision, and sent off in disgrace in the 1982 tournament against Brazil, Maradona finally matured into a complete soccer player in the 1986 World Cup. He was cantankerous, unpredictable, and inconsistent on the field and disastrously self-destructive off it, critics said. He only played a few minutes a game, they said. But in Mexico, he showed that whatever his faults, he could be the greatest player in the game. His speed, ability to go for the goal, and endless craftiness were pivotal to Argentina's winning. Coach Carlos Bilardo's team was not a brilliant side by World Cup standards, but Maradona, who starred for Boca Juniors, Barcelona, and Napoli in his turbulent but record-setting prime, added more than enough of his creative touch to inspire them to greatness. ⚽

FIVE-A-SIDE

From time to time the World Cup has been an incubator of tactical changes in soccer. The 1958 games, for example, brought the world a mature 4–2–4 from the Brazilians. The 1986 games confirmed the increasing role of the midfielder, as the general trend among the successful squads was a five-man midfield. France's Michel Platini, Denmark's Sren Lerby, West Germany's Lothar Matthäus, and England's Glenn Hoddle all were exponents of an elevated midfield responsibility.

France, Germany, Argentina, and Denmark all played with essentially five men across the middle, each of whom had specific creative duties. Diego Maradona generally pushed forward, while Matthäus, with his tireless commitment, generally marked the opponents' star. But in a time when genuine strikers seemed to be few and far between, the five-man midfield reinvigorated the attacking game. ⚽

1990

The 1990 World Cup, staged in soccer-mad Italy, was eagerly anticipated. All of the previous World Cup had champions qualified for the finals. But, when the jury of world opinion was in, the tournament was bereft of the flair and skill which had lent such excitement to pre-

vious editions. Indeed, FIFA itself engaged in much open criticism of referees and of "negative football" which had led to both semifinals being decided on penalty kicks after extra time and to a dismal final that Germany won on a controversial penalty—so typical for this World Cup—in the 85th minute of a poor game.

But Italy's atmosphere and hospitality helped overcome some of the disappointment experienced by fans and other keen observers who had come to expect perhaps too much. The tournament had its high moments—Cameroon's Indomitable Lions toppling defending champion Argentina in the opener and continuing their run right into the quarterfinals; Salvatore "Toto" Schillaci of Italy winning the scoring title and Italian hearts with his daring and his mouth-agape goal celebrations; David Platt's unsighted overhead goal at 119 minutes to pull England past Belgium into the quarterfinals; and Argentina's nation-silencing semifinal defeat of Italy on penalties in steamy Naples.

The tournament was also remarkable for the appearance of the United States, Ireland, and Costa Rica, the latter two for the first time ever. Though the USA's performance was limited, at least the nation which would host the 1994 World Cup had qualified for the tournament on its own and gathered invaluable experience during its two-week first round stay. Ireland and Costa Rica were both in their first World Cup, and made the most of it. With England's World Cup–winning player Jack Charlton as their manager, Ireland reached

the quarterfinals before bowing to Italy. Costa Rica, in an organizational shambles just 40 days prior to the tournament, responded to coach Bora Milutinovic's magic and turned aside Scotland and Sweden en route to the round of sixteen.

After a first round of ties and "games which no one deserved to win," in the words of one coach, the drama finally picked up as the temperatures in summertime Italy soared to above 100 degrees on some days. The round of 16 also produced two classic pairings—West Germany vs. Holland and Argentina vs. Brazil. Argentina survived via a truly magnificent counterattacking through ball from Diego Maradona to striker Claudio Caniggia, while the Germans competed in one of the most memorable games of the tournament, a game played in

Before 'keepers had to master clearances with their feet, Colombia's René Higuita regularly strayed from his area to join the fray; 38-year-old Roger Milla stripped him of the ball and raced in Cameroon's famous winning goal.
(Rogers/Popperfoto)

Tying the game on striker Claudio Caniggia's header, Argentina just overcame Italy, and goalie Walter Zenga (who later played for New England Revolution in MLS), in a penalty shootout after one of the World Cup's tensest semifinal matchups.

(Simon Bruty, Allsport)

120 minutes of 1–1 soccer, Argentina's luck again came through. Italy was eliminated on penalties and the entire host nation was stilled in mourning. The other match, however, was a classic. West Germany and England enraptured Turin with near misses and fierce competition. In the end, however, Germany prevailed via the tiebreaker. The final, matching West Germany and Argentina for the second straight time, was scandalous. Argentina, reeling under suspensions and injuries which deprived them of several starters, made no attempt to attack, clearly hoping that once again their penalty-kick luck would prevail. Referee Edgardo Codesal, however, whistled a penalty on Roberto Sensini in the 84th minute and Brehme struck the winner just beyond the reach of Sergio Goycoechea, who had performed remarkable penalty phase heroics up to then. After two consecutive World Cup Final losses, West Germany finally had its trophy. Maradona stalked the field in tears as Argentina disintegrated in a blur of red cards, finishing with only 9 men. ⚽

Milan, where three of the Germans starred at club level for Internazionale (Milan) and three of the Dutch starred for A.C. Milan. In an exceptionally if predictably intense game, complete with two players sent off, Jürgen Klinsmann put the Germans up after 50 minutes, and Andreas Brehme gave his team an insurmountable lead at 84. The Dutch were out, and Germany was on the march. The quarterfinals continued Argentina's "cardiac kids" style of football. Maradona's mates barely scraped by Yugoslavia on penalties after a scoreless 120 minutes in Florence, while England nearly suffered a humiliation at the feet of Cameroon. The Africans held the lead, 2–1, with just nine minutes remaining, but Cameroon's poise evaporated and two Gary Lineker penalties ended the Lions' run. The semifinals had the makings of high drama, but the first one failed to reach the heights. Argentina and Italy met in Maradona's club's stadium, and for the first time in the tournament Italy could not hold the lead. After a grueling

ITALIA '90   A cynic might say that there were no personalities in the 1990 World Cup and no new tactics to explore. But 1990 was the *Italian* World Cup. Playing under some of the fiercest pressure in sports, the Italian team responded with six wins in seven games, and it was only the luck of penalties that kept the Azzurri from the final. Coach Azeglio Vicini and his team were subjected to daily analysis, praise, castigation, diatribe, and worship depending upon their performance in the previous game. When Gianluca Vialli was amidst a goal-scoring drought, his personal life was spread through the papers as if a national scandal were underway. When Toto Schillaci scored goals, as he did six times in the tournament, the nation rejoiced and beatified the swarthy, relatively unknown Sicilian marksman. Through it all, the Italian team maintained a quiet dignity and marched off with the third-place trophy. The Italians played with style and in the spirit of FIFA's Fair Play guidelines; but for their historically rooted problems with goal scoring, and their Argentine nemesis, they might very well have won. ⚽

FAIR PLAY   The third-place match at the World Cup finals is normally a snooze. But in 1990, it produced some of the most entertaining soccer. England and Italy, both recovering from devastating penalty-kick losses in the semifinals, took the field at Bari with the clear intent of having fun and winning. It was refreshing to the 51,246 in attendance, who thrilled to see Italy win, 2–1. At the game's conclusion—after sharing the victory stand for the medal ceremony—the two teams clowned about and started off on a joint victory lap, saluting fans of both countries. It was a fitting end to Italy's World Cup and was sportsmanship at the highest level. ⚽

1994

World Cup USA 1994 promised the world that it would stage "the greatest World Cup ever and leave a legacy for soccer in the United States." As lofty as those goals may have seemed on their first public utterance in January 1991, they were fulfilled and the tournament earned the praise of FIFA, players, fans worldwide, the American public at large, and the media.

Many observers felt that the tournament was the finest in a quarter century—since the 1970 World Cup in Mexico. Much of the credit for that achievement must, of course, lie with the teams and the players, who rekindled what the immortal Pelé called "the beautiful game."

After a period of doldrums for soccer, of increasingly negative tactics and rough play on the field and hooliganism off it, soccer artistry gloriously reasserted itself at the 1994 World Cup, holding billions of fans in its thrall for the 31-day, 52-game spell. Goal scoring was up, to 2.7 goals per game, reversing a disturbing World Cup trend; individual brilliance abounded, as the genius of Italy's Roberto Baggio, Brazil's Romário, Romania's Georghe Hagi, and Bulgaria's Hristo Stoichkov continually left commentators gasping for descriptive phrases; unheralded teams gave exciting performances, notably South Korea and Saudi Arabia; and fans of all nations celebrated the World Cup together without a single disreputable incident.

Despite an unusually hot summer, which saw temperatures in each venue above 90 degrees, the play was energetic and creative throughout. It was Italy who provided many of the heart-stopping moments of the tournament. The Azzurri, battling a mounting list of injuries as the month wore on, came close to tumbling twice, but the Divine Ponytail–the long-locked Roberto Baggio—thrice saved them. Reminiscent of 1982, Italy barely reached the knockout phase—but then came alive. Italy was upset in its opening match against Ireland and the boo-birds were out in force, heaping abuse on coach Arrigo Sacchi and his players. It barely got any better in the group matches, but with a 1–0 win against an uninspired Norway (Baggio was surprisingly pulled in the first half when a red card on goalkeeper Pagliuca reduced Italy to ten men; his namesake, Dino Baggio, scored the winner) and a tie against Mexico, Italy advanced, and Roberto Baggio's table was set for greatness. In the Round of 16, Roberto's two goals–one in the 88th minute and one in overtime–put Italy past a stubborn and talented Nigeria; in the quarterfinals it was an 87th-minute pearl of a shot against a strong Spanish team on the verge of overwhelming the Italians which eased the skids into the semifinals, where the 27-year-old Juventus star and 1993 FIFA footballer of the year struck twice again.

Amidst the Italian last-ditch

The 1994 World Cup finale: Brazil's victorious goalkeeper Claudio Taffarel and Italy's striker Roberto Baggio graphically express their emotions after the injured Baggio misses his penalty kick in the 3–2 shootout.

(Mike Powell, Allsport)

recoveries, there was the saga of Diego Maradona, soccer's bad boy, which came to a sad climax when he was banned from the '94 tournament for illegal substance abuse. A half-fit Maradona had been recalled to rescue the national team as it struggled to reach the tournament finals at all. He led—though some said he more often walked—the team through a play-off against Australia but appeared in full form for his opening tournament game, a 4–0 thrashing of nouveaux arrivistes Greece. After some brilliant performances, most notably a 2–1 showcase of his skills against Nigeria—in which there were times when twenty-one players waited in anticipation of his next move—he tested positive. Though the case was as controversial as all sports doping cases are, the spark of Argentina's team was banned by FIFA and the Argentine federation, ending the teams hopes—Argentina lost immediately to Bulgaria and to Romania--and Maradona's international career. The dark horse of the tournament was Bulgaria, which survived a first-round group that included Nigeria and Argentina, upended Mexico on penalty kicks, and then dismissed the defending champions Germany to produce the surprise of the competition. The hard-working Emil Kostadinov and Iordan Letchkov combined with Stoichkov, a player seemingly capable of playing any, indeed every, field position for his side during the course of a game, to stage a memorable 2–1 comeback against a German team laden with the experience and talents of Klinsmann, Matthäus, Völler, Möller, and Hässler.

Brazil, thought by many to have its finest team ever, rather quietly did its job, reaching the final undefeated and suffering just one tie, that in a meaningless group match. Romário and fellow scorer Bebeto, defenders Jorginho and Aldair, midfielders Branco and Dunga, the surehanded Taffarel, et. al., blended into a marvelously efficient soccer machine that scored 11 goals and surrendered only 3, a powerful demonstration that Brazilians had finally learned how to defend. Total dominance was the result.

While Brazil was progressing to its fourth World Cup, records were set for attendance and television ratings. More than 3.5 million fans poured through the turnstiles of America's nine venues and television ratings in the United States broke all previous marks for soccer viewership. Indeed, ABC's research department calculated that more than 40 million Americans watched all or part of the classic USA–Brazil match, held on the Fourth of July. The game began excitingly enough as German-born USA citizen Thomas Dooley skimmed the post with a fine shot; but Brazil, though reduced to ten men after midfielder Leonardo was

Roy Keane blocks Italy's Giuseppe Signori, in the 1–0 Irish first round victory. In a stadium newly turfed and wrapped in green flags, Ireland revenged their 1990 loss. The future finalist had to regroup after the initial shock.

(Bob Thomas/Popperfoto)

Though both teams met with frustration (Romania fell on penalties in '90 and '94; Colombia on miscues), since 1990 Romania's Georghe Hagi and Colombia's Carlos Valderrama graced the Cup with attractive skills and off-balance playmaking.

(Shaun Botterill, Allsport)

sent off for a vicious elbowing of USA playmaker Tab Ramos, simply wore down the Americans and left little doubt as to their unmatchable superiority—at full complement or not. The American team had done well, creating enormous popular interest after beating Colombia in stylish fashion and producing several heroes–Alexi Lalas, Marcelo Balboa, Tony Meola, and Ernie Stewart, in particular. Perhaps even more remarkable is the fact that the World Cup Final, held in the Rose Bowl, without of course the United States as a participant, drew a higher USA television rating than the USA–Brazil game (9.5 to 9.3).

The American media, long a thorn to many soccer devotees because of its seeming disinterest in the sport, went head over heels for the tournament. Nothing could state this better than a comment from the *Washington Post*'s poetic baseball writer Thomas Boswell, writing in the June 29 edition about a relatively obscure first round game: "Belgium plays Saudi Arabia at RFK Stadium this afternoon. . . .Take a tip from a friend. Find a way to go. Sometimes, the thing itself proves to be as good as the hype. That's true of the World Cup." Other converts wrote similar columns coast to coast as the World Cup made front-page news for the duration of the tournament.

The final was more chess match than soccer game, as the two teams, each seeking their fourth world title, feinted and probed for 120 minutes. Romário's signature surges straight up the middle of the defense were collapsed by the equally skillful defending of Paolo Maldini and Franco Barese; Baggio was left to shoot from long distance.

As fitting for these closely matched sides as it might have been frustrating, the game moved inexorably to penalties. Clearly feeling the pressure and exhausted by the heat, three Italians and two Brazilians out of the first five missed, including Italy's two most celebrated players, Barese and Baggio. Brazil claimed a cup they truly had won outright over the month's campaign. ⚽

BAGGIO BELLISSIMO

In a World Cup which saw many shining examples of individual achievement, Roberto Baggio was the man of the month. The pony-tailed Italian sex symbol shook off injuries and took charge of Italy's fortunes, just as Paolo Rossi had done in 1982. The devotee of Zen found great inner strength, scoring five of Italy's six knock-out phase goals–and almost all his were magical goals, conjured from seemingly nothing–leading the team directly to the final. Two against Nigeria, one against Spain, two against Bulgaria, and Italy was in the final. Yes, he missed the final kick of the California afternoon; but it must be remembered a successful shot would only have tied the game. All in all no one could have asked or received more of one player over 31 days. ⚽

WHAT PRICE VICTORY?

The summer of '94 was one of soccer joy; but it had a moment of tragedy which serves as a boldface footnote. The USA's 2–1 win over Colombia may have been the most compelling upset of the 52-game marathon, but the human dimension was not to be known until days later. Though the USA fully deserved the victory, the opening American goal came from the foot of Colombian defender Andres Escobar, who accidentally put the ball past his goalkeeper, Oscar Cordoba. The defeat put Colombia—a team with Valderrama, Rincon, and Asprilla—out of the tournament they'd hoped would improve their country's reputation in America. Instead, they left with heads bowed, a squad in disarray. Worse was to come. Only days after, Escobar was shot to death in his native country in a dispute related to the unfortunate own goal. ⚽

Late in a close team effort, USA players celebrate Ernie Stewart's game-winning goal in their 2–1 victory over Colombia, delivering the team into the second round.
(Dave Cannon, Allsport)

ONLY IN AMERICA

For the 1984 Olympic Games in Los Angeles, Alan Rothenberg was appointed commissioner of soccer by the Los Angeles Organizing Committee. Perhaps no one other than Rothenberg anticipated the stirring success soccer would be at that Games. Soccer in America had suffered a dramatic decline as the N.A.S.L. gradually dissolved, with Rothenberg's own Los Angeles Aztecs franchise a victim too of the league's demise. Moreover, soccer was not traditionally so popular at the Olympics: since the 1950s, the sport's powers either did not compete or sent teams of players under 23 years of age.

Yet the matches at the Rose Bowl outdrew all other Olympic sports, and more than 105,000 people—the largest crowd to that date to watch a soccer game in North America—filled the Rose Bowl for the Olympic gold medal match, between France and Brazil.

Rothenberg, whose soccer education began as general manager of the humble L. A. Wolves of the USSA, now lobbied FIFA for the game's biggest prize. Missing out to Mexico in 1986 meant waiting until 1994 (as the Cup returned to Europe). When the wait was over, undreamed-of numbers of soccer aficionados and newcomers to the game alike filled every stadium for almost every match, feasting on the best the game can offer. ⚽

Crunch time in the 1994 World Cup Final: Brazil's captain, Dunga, and Italy's Roberto Baggio crash to earth in front of lauded referee Sandor Puhl.
(Bob Thomas, Popperfoto)

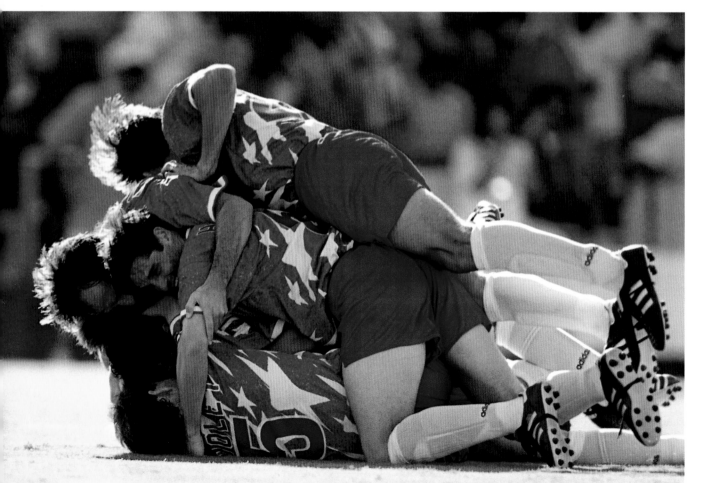

DESTINATION FRANCE 1998
ELIO TRIFARI

What has really changed since you and a couple of billion people watched the last World Cup? Perhaps, in fact, nothing at all has changed? The game in town is still Europe vs. South America, as it was since the first Jules Rimet Trophy (now FIFA World Cup) was awarded to Uruguay in 1930. Yet soccer is evolving from a game known only to two-thirds of the world to a global game. Television expansion is the principal reason for this, but TV could soon be a force that actually restricts the game's popularity and visibility in the near future. As interest grows, matches of great intrinsic value will succumb to video-on-demand opportunities.

It's still the same old game, we say. After 643 matches have been played over 18 months to select from 172 entrants the 32 countries who will animate the 16th edition of World Cup, the question is still the same: Europe or South America? In fact, after sixty years of competition, only six of the almost two hundred "countries" included in FIFA's membership (some of them are in political reality small territories without independent administration) have won the World Cup; all but Uruguay will be in France.

In the past, the confrontation of European and South American powers was always shaped, superficially at least, as one of virtuosity vs. organization: but soccer frontiers have been broken in the last dozen years to such an extent that it's rare to find a Brazilian or Argentine national-calibre player who is not under contract to a European club. And there are a lot of coaches from both continents (though of the 32 head coaches of the qualifiers for France, 5 are Brazilians) traveling the world offering advice to established and to emerging countries' federations, blending club, national, even regional trends into an international mélange.

Mexico, strong in '98, as in '94, went undefeated in CONCACAF qualifying and won the 1996 Gold Cup. Pavel Pardo leads the team out to play Ecuador in the 1997 Copa America.
(Mark Thompson, Allsport)

You could still name Brazil as the greatest foundry of talent in the world and be correct—but its stadiums are far from replete with the famous *torcida* of fans and only mirages of rich European contracts and the support of multinational sponsors prevent the home of Pelé and Ronaldo from becoming a second-class soccer country, the fate that has befallen Uruguay—once a leader in talent and game organization—and Peru, also excluded from the Big Show in France. Even if you can look at Brazil as a real force on the field, it's difficult for most fans to name more than two or three stars from Argentina, the only other established South American power.

The ball is really in Europe's fields. Clubs and federations feed the game with money, analyses, tactical seminars—and see these innovations, rather than local initiatives, returning as the soul of newcomers' games. Thus, while enlarging the panorama to 32 countries for France has resulted in several abso-

lute surprises—Jamaica and Iran, notably—and some welcome strong additions—South Africa and Yugoslavia both rejoin the soccer world after political bans—it is unlikely to modify the balance of power. The Arab world has several entrants, too, but Europe is soccer's mecca, judging by the wealth of its leading clubs, playing opportunities, attendance, or—the most important thing today—visibility. TV rights are growing along an impressive curve, becoming the greatest share of a club's revenue in Britain (whose clubs are also very strong in merchandising) and Spain, while Germany, France, and Italy, which started pay television a little later, are now experiencing their first relevant results.

It has to be said that there has been little evolution in tactics in the last four years. A match involving two European teams—even if one has a man-to-man manager, the other a firm zonal evangelist—is now tactically very pre-

Left: Heading to France '98: Mexico's Ricardo Pelaez and Carlos Hermosillo shut out tiny St. Vincent, 5–0.
(David Leah, Allsport)

Above: England and Martin Keown climbed above Mexico and "Zaque" Alves in a 1997 2–0 friendly international (exhibition) match.
(Popperfoto)

*Left: South Africa's Lucas Radebe clears from Tunisia's Slimane Medhi in the 2–0
African Nations Cup Final; both teams qualified for France.*

(Mark Thompson, Allsport)

Below: Brazil sent England literally head over heels, winning 3–1 in the 1995 Umbro Cup.

(David Cannon, Allsport)

*Right: Morocco's Nourredine Naybet helped lead his nation, whose Raja team won the 1997
African Champions League, over Ghana, 1–0, and to their second World Cup finals.*

(Clive Brunskill, Allsport)

dictable. The players and coaches now know each other well from the international-ization of the rosters of domestic clubs and from the expand-ed European competitions. Fans hoping for more open matches thus wait with anticipation for African, Asian, or CONCACAF teams to interrupt the expected program. Nigeria, 1996 Olympic champion, will be a formidable opponent—but innovative? Its leading players are all established at major European clubs. Europe's traditional powers, a tough if aging Germany and Holland and the back-to-defensive-playing Italy, join host France, newly sophisticated England, and Spain as expected contenders. Abundantly talented Romania, Bulgaria, Croatia, and Yugoslavia (the Czechs and Russians surprisingly stumbling), like Norway and Denmark, send their players into the major Western European leagues. But the World Cup finals is al-most always good for sur-prises, so we shall keenly wait to see who is willing to be inventive and imaginative.

And the United States? Surely soccer is gaining popularity in schools and colleges across the country, but it has not dug roots yet into the entire population. When this second revo-lution comes, then certainly America will have the expertise and resources to match—the 2010 plan is in place to make the USA a world power. Perhaps black Americans will join the sport in great numbers, adding to a rising number of black stars all around the world. We'll have to wait and see—if we can. Most say the next World Cup—unusually scheduled for 2002 in two countries, Japan and South Korea—will probably show their best games on pay-per-view or personalized broadcasting. We must take heart that at the same time soccer will probably be played more widely than ever on the world's streets—it's too easy to be only a game for the filthy rich. ⚽

Surprises all!

One-way traffic: Yugoslavia's Dejan Savicevic (in white) and Predrag Mijatovic (who led the qualifying rounds with 14 goals) were tripped only by Spain's Sergi and Nadal in qualifying. Both nations are now major European forces.

(Popperfoto)

Bundesliga striker Khodadad Azizi gave Iran unexpected soccer fever by a record-breaking 17–0 win over tiny Maldives, then by tying Australia in Melbourne in the final World Cup qualifying play-off match for France '98. In Teheran, 70,000 people met the returning team, including 3,000 women defying religious prohibitions against their attendance.

(Allsport)

In a fierce Asian qualifying competition, Japan's Norio Omura is tackled by South Korea's Yong-Su Choi. Both the 2002 World Cup finals host nations qualified for France, Japan for the very first time.

(Ben Radford, Allsport)

Giant-killers Jamaica, led by Deon Burton, one of the four London-born so-called Reggae Boyz, tied the USA in Washington and then sent their celebrating nation to its first World Cup finals.

(Jamie Squire, Allsport)

The key moment in the USA's qualification for France '98: Tab Ramos, back from career-threatening injury, celebrates his winning goal late in the 1–0 victory over Costa Rica, in Portland.

(J. B. Whitesell, ISI)

Phantom soccer: Scotland kicks off without Estonia, which boycotted its 1996 home World Cup qualifying match after a dispute about suitable match conditions. Scotland unsurprisingly "won" three seconds later, but the long arm of FIFA ordered a rematch, which ended 0–0.
(Ben Radford, Allsport)

Captained by goalie José-Luis Chilavert, Paraguay lifted itself into second place in South America and qualification for France '98.
(David Leah, Allsport)

MAJOR LEAGUE SOCCER

The historic moment came before 31,683 fans at Spartan Stadium, as the San Jose Clash beat D. C. United, 1–0, on April 6, 1996, in the first Major League Soccer game. Fittingly, USA forward Eric Wynalda scored the league's first goal. ("Thank God for Wynalda," breathed one official, relieved that a scoreless tie had been avoided.) And interest was clearly piqued: on June 16, 1996, an astounding 92,260 spectators watched the fast-starting L. A. Galaxy play the Tampa Bay Mutiny. The crowd was there in force to celebrate the game in America. Two years after the magical 1994 World Cup, first-class soccer was back.

And back with a stated mandate: to encourage attacking, entertaining soccer and to improve the performance of U. S. club, national, and youth teams in international competition. The scoring is there: an average of 3.3 goals per game is higher than in most leagues, perhaps encouraged by the shootout fate befalling a game tied at the end of regulation time. In 1997, 33 games were decided by shootout. Establishing the grass roots is considered vital to the league's success, as the lack of a fan and player base has been considered the critical factor in the demise of the N.A.S.L. Thus, there is MLS and USSF's "Project 40" that identifies top young soccer talent and provides training opportunities and a five-year academic package awarded by USSF.

MLS has attracted outstanding coaches, from Brazilian Carlos Alberto Parreira, whose four trips to the World Cup (1982–98) include his victorious 1994 Brazil team, to American Bruce Arena, whose Virginia teams dominated NCAA Division I and whose winning ways have worked well for two-time MLS champs, D. C. United.

Fittingly, too, home-grown talent has decided the first two championships . In '96 Eddie Pope's winning "golden goal" secured the first MLS trophy for D. C. United in its 3–2 win over the Galaxy at Foxboro. At RFK in '97, United triumphed over the Rapids, 2–1, with a winning goal from Tony Sanneh. In 1997, United was also the league's top-scoring team. ⚽

Keeping 15 of 20 spots on the roster for home-grown talent, MLS has delivered a number of new stars to the soccer world. National team striker Roy Lassiter has been a prolific scorer for the Tampa Bay Mutiny.
(Scott Indermaur, MLS/Allsport)

At Mile High Stadium, Rapids' Marcelo Balboa goes
aerial with D. C. United's David Vaudreuil in a 5–2
loss early in the '97 season; both teams made it
to the second MLS championship game.

(Brian Bahr, MLS/Allsport)

Most of the U. S. national team stayed home, or came home,
to make MLS a success:

Chris Henderson's 87th-minute goal took the
Colorado Rapids to the 1997 MLS Cup Final.
(Eric Bakke, MLS/Allsport)

Eric Wynalda returned from the Bundesliga to score
MLS's first goal for the San Jose Clash.
(John Todd, MLS/Allsport)

New England Revolution's Joe-Max Moore is the third-leading scorer in USA team history.
(David Silverman, MLS/Allsport)

The overall first draft choice in 1996, Brian McBride performed outstandingly for the Columbus Crew and earned his stripes for the USA team.
(Greg Bartram, MLS/Allsport)

National team stalwart Cobi Jones scored the franchise's first goal and spearheaded the L. A. Galaxy to a second-place finish in 1996.
(Jamie Squire, MLS/Allsport)

Paying respect to the influence of his haberdashery, at least, the Kansas City Wizards line up for a game with Valderrama and the Mutiny in 1996 in Tampa Stadium.

(Andy Lyons, Allsport)

Valderrama's impact on young aspirants is seen at home and away—as here at Mile High Stadium before a Colorado Rapids–Mutiny game.

(Stephen Dunn, Allsport)

LATIN LESSONS
RIGOBERTO CERVANTEZ

Noted for creatively "spraying passes" throughout a game, Carlos "Pibe" Valderrama is one of the world's most elegant playmakers. 1996 league MVP for Tampa Bay Mutiny, he joined Miami Fusion at the end of 1997. Valderrama led Colombia to the 1990, 1994, and 1998 World Cup finals and was South American footballer of the year in 1987 and 1993.

(Andy Lyons, Allsport)

In U. S. soccer history, it is easy to find such names as Garcia, Mendoza, Borjas, Ramos, and other Latino or Hispanic players. But have Hispanics helped in unique ways to enhance the American game's profile? The answers add up to a resounding yes.

Hispanics officials and organizers have raised the game's infrastructure in this country, from youth to professional levels. The Hispanic media for many years has been *the* beacon for soccer, sending out a constant flow of information about the national and international game. The excitement such commentators as Andrés Cantor (he of the much-imitated "gooooooal" refrain) bring is one of soccer's thrills for Americans of all tongues.

The loyalty that Hispanics have for the game has greatly helped MLS, as Hispanic stars created instant followings in Latino communities. National coach Steve Sampson has rightly taken advantage of his fluent Spanish to ask for similar support for the U. S. team—and one should note the U. S. team has long had names like Columbos, Matas, and Souza (who all played in the 1950 upset of England) on its roster.

Hispanics are loyal to the game. In the '70s and '80s, Hispanic players populated much of the development programs and amateur leagues. Hugo Salcedo, for example, a native of Jalisco, in Mexico, came to the U. S. at a very young age and became a citizen while at U.C.L.A. He developed his game in the California Soccer League and was on the 1972 Olympic team. His son Jorge currently plays for Columbus Crew.

Certainly the Latino player has greatly advantaged the national team. The team naturally draws on a melting pot of talents and style, but Bora Milutinovic, a European with a Latino soccer mentality, realized that if he could combine European-style players with those who grew up with the Latino touch and dribbling talents, he could compete with the best. He encouraged players to be adaptable, asking Marcelo Balboa, Fernando Clavijo, Hugo Perez, and Tab Ramos to change the pace of the game from predictable long-balls to short-passing ball control and to improvise. This allowed the U. S. team to have different ways to approach each match.

So, yes, the Hispanic game has contributed to the enrichment and growth of U. S. soccer. After all, it's part of America's culture. ⚽

Along with Valderrama, Hispanic players such as El Salvador's and L. A. Galaxy's Mauricio Cienfuegos and those shown here have given MLS instant support and credibility.

Mexico's and Chicago Fire's goalkeeper Jorge Campos led Mexico to the 1994 and 1998 World Cup finals. He sometimes plays as a forward and has scored several goals, one of which was in MLS play.

(Pam Friend, ISI)

Bolivia's and D. C. United's Marco Etcheverry, in the 1997 MLS Cup Final, passes Sean Henderson, Colorado Rapids. Etcheverry played in the 1994 World Cup finals.

(Stephen Dunn, Allsport)

Bolivia's and D. C. United's Jaime Moreno, with
Colorado Rapids' Peter Vermes.

(J. B. Whitesell, ISI)

El Salvador's and D. C. United's Raul Diaz Arce, tackled
by Cle Kooiman, Tampa Bay Mutiny.

(Tony Quinn, Allsport)

SAM'S ARMY IS SINGING!

"Swing low, sweet chariot, coming for to carry me home. . ."—*spiritual sung by English soccer fans at moments of great tension in games.*

At Italia '90, as "flares and sparklers popped and burned . . .colored smoke drifted through the sea of swaying flags," American player Bruce Murray said to Pete Davies, "We don't have the fan base—I think it'll take another ten years at least." But the zealots have arrived—a.k.a. Sam's Army, the unofficial fan club of the national team that has been growing in number since World Cup USA—another step in making the U. S. soccer experience complete. An overflow crowd for the 1997 Costa Rica game wrapped the Portland stadium in banners and, led by the red-shirted Army, chanted continuously, building to a euphoric climax with Ramos' winning goal.

Like American soccer itself, Sam's Army melds influences from around the world: the as-you-go instrumental and percussion accompaniment of Latin American crowds, the rhythmic chants of Italian fans, and the well-known English fans' rousing anthems—many of which are derived from pop music. If the passion is one decibel below the intimidating power of Barcelona's Nou Camp, the riotous, nonstop frenzy of Argentina's River Plate stadium, or the full-throated singing at England's Wembley, it is because, at heart, American sports fans are gregarious and sociable, more like Scandinavia's "*roligans*."

Thankfully, hooliganism, the dangerous blight of the sport in the '80s, has been systematically marginalized, and stadiums in Europe, in the wake of several disasters in the '80s and early '90s, have been dramatically upgraded. Fan power, with real fans expressing concerns about the way the sport is being run in fanzines and on the web, is now an organized, voluble force that characterizes soccer the world over. ⚽

Top row, left and right: two of the more colorful Azzurri (Italian national team) tifosi, one revealing loyalty to her club (Juventus), the other to her idol. Center: Fans bring the Cameroon magic.
Middle row, left to right: Barcelona fan in club and Catalonian colors; Moroccan supporter; dancers from the Brazilian torcida.
Bottom row, left to right: None more representative: Euro '96 fans from Spain, Germany, and England.
Above: A member of the Tartan Army is resigned to another of Scotland's excruciating first-round exits.
(Top row, left and right: Richiardi; Top center, Popperfoto; Middle row, left to right: Richiardi, Allsport, Popperfoto; Bottom row: all photos, Richiardi; Above: Clive Brunskill, Allsport)

As the world over,
the USA national team now
has passionate, organized, enviable support.
Above and right: Peruvian and Norwegian fans.
(Left: Mark Thompson, Allsport; Center: J. B. Whitesell, ISI; Right: Richiardi)

FAIR PLAY AND
WITH VINNIE MAURO

Left: Mugging around: Norway's Jan Aage Fjortoft shares a little extra Fair Play respect with England's Tim Flowers.
(Clive Brunskill, Allsport)

Top: Liberia's George Weah, 1995 FIFA player of the year, tries out some points on the referee in a 2–0 World Cup qualifying loss to Tunisia.
(Clive Brunskill, Allsport)

Right: Germany's Jürgen Klinsmann mugs his way round Spain's Albert Ferrer during World Cup '94.
(Ben Radford, Allsport)

FOUL

An initiative undertaken in 1988, the Fair Play doctrine is a touchstone of modern soccer. FIFA annually puts significant financial resources behind the campaign and the words "Fair Play" are elements of nearly every communication from FIFA officials. Fair Play is an all-encompassing concept, involving respect and ethical standards of clean competition between players, between players and referees, and between opposing fans, including accepting defeat with dignity. FIFA annually honors a player with the Fair Play Award at its yearly banquet in January. Recipients have been players who have shown exemplary actions on the field and in their community, perhaps most notably Jacques Glassmann, a French player who uncovered a match-fixing scandal.

FIFA has done much recently to remove cynicism from the game: discouraging the "professional foul," red-carding the last defender if he prevents an obvious scoring opportunity, as well as yellow-carding players who overdramatize being fouled, and invoking more liberal offside rules to favor attackers. In addition FIFA is evaluating refs more carefully than ever, and involving the referee's assistants more in the running of the game. Still fans bemoan refs, but there is something sacred about the subjective, human element. As long-suffering fan Nick Hornby has written, "outrageously bad refereeing decisions" are among the basic elements needed "for a match to be truly memorable. Indignation is a crucial ingredient of the perfect footballing experience. . . .I prefer to howl at [refs], to feel cheated by them. . .as long as they don't cost us the match."

Of course, knowing really what the players and refs say to each other is a secret a little like knowing what a Scotsman wears under his kilt. U. S. soccer had a superb, world-class referee in Vinnie Mauro. He officiated in 17 tournaments for FIFA and CONCACAF, including the 1990 World Cup finals, 1988 Olympic Games, 1989 Asian Games, 1989 Copa America, the first CONCACAF Gold Cup, and each of the CONCACAF U-17 and U-20 tournaments from 1986 to 1991. He retired in 1998 after a career of memorable experiences that shed light on what a ref really says—and on what he chooses to see:

"During the Pelé Cup in 1991 I was assigned to the Italy vs. Argentina match. I didn't tell anybody I could speak Italian. As a referee this is part of the game, and besides nobody asked me. During the match I called a foul on the Italian center forward. Well, he addressed me with a few four-letter words in Italian, so when he finally got close enough to where I could speak quietly to him, I said to him in Italian, 'Hey, why are we Italians always making ourselves noticeable on the field.' His face turned immediately white. When the half ended he came over and apologized to me for five minutes.

"The same thing happened to me during the 1988 Olympics. I was the fourth official for the Italy–USSR match. The Italian bench knew I could speak Italian as I had told them, but not the players on the field. In the second half, USSR went ahead 2–1 and the

Above: Not so fast? England's David Beckham is redirected by Italy's Demetrio Albertini in a 1997 World Cup qualifying match.
(Stu Forster, Allsport)

Left: Italy's Alessandro Nesta keeps France's Christophe Dugarry out of harm's way in the 1997 Tournoi de France.
(TempSport, Richiardi)

tension on the field became very high. An Italian player went down injured but the referee didn't acknowledge the doctors and this infuriated one of the Italian players on the field, who came over shouting profanities at me. The Italian bench then went berserk trying to signal the irate player to tell him that I understood what he was saying. But I politely said to him in Italian, 'You can scream at me as loud as you want, but it's the referee who will allow the doctors onto the field.' With that, the shocked player calmly turned and walked away, never saying another word.

"Another incident happened several years ago while I was officiating an amateur match in Massachusetts. During the match I sent off a tall defender for a bad tackle. As he's walking off the field and I'm writing his number in my book, I get shoved in the back. I turn around and it's the same guy that I just sent off, only now he's fully dressed in normal clothes. And my first thought is, 'Wait a second, this guy just walked the other way wearing a uniform.' But then I realized that it was the guy's twin brother. Not only that but he was a player who was watching the match because he was serving a suspension!"

Vinnie, like all good referees, prefers his own anonymity: "The Brazil–Paraguay match in the 1989 Copa America was pressured. Brazil was at home and needed a victory to move on in the tournament. The press was asking why an American was refereeing this match. In fact, one CONCACAF official said something to me before the match that I'll always remember. He said, 'You'll live or die in the middle of the field today.' His point was that the image of CONCACAF was resting on my shoulders. So you know that there was pressure. The match went very smoothly, and as I walked off the field it was an incredible feeling because I knew in my heart that I had done a good job. The next day the people were not talking about the American referee, but rather the performance of the Brazilians. It's best when they don't talk about the referee. . . ." ⚽

Above: Trapping the man, if not the ball: Ireland's Jason McAteer is ensnared in a 0–3 loss to Portugal.
(Ross Kinnaird, Allsport)

Right: Off and running? Holland's Winston Bogarde finds only one way to stop England's Euro '96–leading scorer, Alan Shearer.
(Popperfoto)

*Not tickled, Italy's and Middlesbrough's Fabrizio "the White Feather"
Ravanelli (right; now playing at Olympique Marseille) has a tête-à-tête
with Ireland's and Aston Villa's Steve Staunton.*
(Anton Want, Allsport)

*Two of the world's best: Germany's Thomas Hässler and Italy's
Gianfranco Zola show a touch of sportsmanship.*

(Popperfoto)

Mano-a-mano, Brazil's Roberto Carlos, Italy's Alessandro Costacurta, and the referee exemplify Fair Play in the 1997 Tournoi de France.
(Shaun Botterill, Allsport)

USA teammates Preki Radosavljevic, 1997 MLS player of the year, and Alexi Lalas share some choice words during a 1997 MLS game between the Kansas City Wizards and the New England Revolution.
(Stephen Dunn, Allsport)

Down to the last 8: Croatia's Slaven Bilic shows no quarter to Christian Ziege during a 1–2 loss to Germany in a Euro '96 quarterfinal game.
(Bob Thomas, Popperfoto)

PENALTY!

The penalty shootout's "worst defect," wrote Hugh McIlvanney, "is that it distorts a team game into an ordeal for individuals in isolation." As he wrote about England and Italy, which both lost semifinal shootouts in the '90 World Cup, "They had not even committed the offense of losing a football match. But neither had the hosts [Italy] and they, too, found themselves sitting on the curb holding their heads—and wondering how the hell they ever stood for such house rules." Perhaps because even a penalty after a blatant foul is something of a foreign concept to soccer—a contrived, unspontaneous shot (though FIFA now allows goalies to move along the goal line before the ball is actually struck), the idea of settling great scores with a shootout is one of soccer's most anguished dilemmas. If a match decided by a regulation penalty is a little tainted, winning one on penalties footnotes the game itself. FIFA has now introduced the golden goal, or sudden death, and there are calls for reducing the number of players on the field during extra-time. MLS has at least a balanced shootout, requiring a player to attack the goal by dribbling from 35 yards within 5 seconds with the goalie allowed off his line to stop him. But undeniably penalty shootouts are a time of the most memorable emotion. As Roddy Doyle wrote about the finale to Ireland–Romania in 1990: "The players sat and stood in the center circle and tried to look like they weren't terrified. . .We had to score our last one. . . David O'Leary, a great player and a nice man. . .No one spoke. He placed the ball. It took him ages. . .It hit the net in a way that was gorgeous. I cried." ⚽

High noon in Kingston, Jamaica: his wall in place, Kasey Keller
awaits a direct kick during the spring 1997 World Cup qualifying
international match.
(Simon Bruty, Any Chance?)

All in a day's work: Keller in action vs. Sunderland and in training for Leicester City in 1997; celebrating victory over Costa Rica in the 1997 World Cup qualifying game. As Camus wrote, playing goal taught him life's lessons, "as the ball never came to you where you'd expect it," and often it came accompanied with "shin−massage with boots, shirt pulled back by the hand, knees in the distinguished parts, sandwiches against the post. . .in brief, a scourge."

(Left: J.B. Whitesell, ISI; center: Gary Mortimore, Allsport; right: Popperfoto)

Acrobatic and quick when necessary, superb in the air at all times, and defiantly capable of making space for himself when threatened by forwards, Keller has honed his art on the international stage and by tutoring himself in the English League, in which a fast-paced, physically demanding aerial game has produced a long tradition of great goalkeepers, including World Cup heroes Gordon Banks and Peter Shilton, as well as current stars Jim Leighton (Scotland's 'keeper, who is about to compete in his fourth World Cup finals), Australia's Mark Bosnich, Norway's Peter Grodas and Erik Thorstvedt, Denmark's Peter Schmeichel, and England's own David Seaman, hero of the Euro '96 campaign.

Keller, of course, is not your average student. His current accomplishments over the past six-and-a-half years in the English professional league are simply mind-boggling. He has started in more professional games than any other U.S. player who has ventured across the Atlantic to ply the trade—a lineage that includes Roy Wegerle, Cobi Jones, John Harkes (the first American ever to play in a Cup Final at Wembley), Tab Ramos, Claudio Reyna, Eric Wynalda, and Jovan Kirovski—by a long shot. Harkes and Wegerle were established players in England before returning to the USA team for 1994 and then going on to MLS teams. Ramos played for Real Betis in Spain, and Kirovski has played for two of Europe's greatest clubs, Manchester United and Borussia Dortmund. But Keller has averaged 50 starts for six seasons in England, a total of more than 300 competitive games, more than double the next closest American.

He began his professional career in 1991 at First Division Millwall, a blue-collar, southeast London club. Millwall is not England's most glamorous club, by a long stretch, but the club has a tradition of playing very hard and a long list of alumni who graduated to play for some of England's greatest teams. The fans, too, are renowned country-wide for the intensity of their support, and it is most fitting that the compact stadium, which reaches intimidating levels of noise on

KEEPING GOAL
WITH KASEY KELLER

The United States has been blessed with a truly excellent goalkeeper: though it took him several years to secure the number-one position for the national team, Kasey Keller is now one of the world's most polished performers. He has that most important of goalkeeping attributes: he gives his defense confidence, because he marshals them well and because he seems so sure of himself. Keller's confident—almost arrogant—control of his area, seen throughout Copa America '95 and the World Cup France qualifying matches, is his trademark.

Saturday afternoons, is known as the Den.

Keller reached hero status at Millwall after the First Division team tied Premier team Chelsea in a 1993 F. A. Cup game at home and then beat them away in a penalty shootout to go through to the next round. Shortly after, however, Kasey was transferred from Millwall to Leicester City, a club in the Midlands of England, and life in the Premier Division (and into a much publicized tug-of-war for his services between the USA team, which FIFA insists can call up a player 7 times in a season for international duty, and Leicester).

Playing in the Premier means he has kept goal for Leicester at Liverpool's famed Anfield stadium, at Manchester United's Old Trafford, and at Arsenal's Highbury. But most important, he has played at Wembley, where Leicester beat Middlesbrough, whose strikers included Italy's Fabrizio Ravanelli and Brazil's Juninho, to win the League (or Coca-Cola) Cup in 1997. This meant Leicester, traditionally a small club with limited ambition, now joined some of the giants of the game in European competition in 1998. Spain's star-studded Atletico Madrid pushed Leicester out of the '97–98 UEFA Cup competition, but the club, under experienced Martin O'Neill, a much decorated player in his days at Nottingham Forest in the 1970s, has shown it can at least challenge England's and Europe's best teams.

"The one thing that has benefited me the most from playing so long in England is the competition," Keller has said. "Every time you step onto the field you know you can easily get your butt kicked.

"It doesn't happen in college and it doesn't happen right now in the MLS. You have to perform in Europe and if you don't they'll go out and buy someone else to replace you, simple as that. They'll scour the earth to find someone."

The difference between English and U.S. soccer, according to Keller, is in many ways the intensity. Keller alludes to four areas where this hypothesis

holds true: training sessions, the fans, the media, and the youth players. "I'm not saying that the U.S. is going about this all wrong. I'm saying that there is something to be learned from both perspectives."

Keller is considered by many to be a perfect trainer. Not in the sense that he never makes a mistake, but more in his focused approach. His college coach Clive Charles (University of Portland), who also doubles as the U. S. National Team assistant coach says, "Kasey is the most focused soccer player I have ever seen in the United States." He simply enjoys training. Hard. And he does not like to waste time.

"I like to break down my game and work on one element, fine tune it and get out," he says. He does not watch game tapes. And he does not do needless drills, like somersaults before catching the ball. "I like to do things as game-related as possible."

"I often see the young goalkeepers at U. S. camps working on certain advanced things when they can't even catch a ball. If you can't catch a ball two feet away, how can you possibly expect to catch one four feet away."

And for the coaches who like to drop the ball from their hands and volley at their goalkeepers, Keller replies, "How many times have you seen a forward pick up a ball and volley it in for a goal. It does not happen that way, so why do it?"

Keller's approach is intense, efficient, and, most of all, effective.

'Keeping it out—Keller and his peers:
(J. B. Whitesell, ISI)

Top: Holland's Edwin Van der Saar, 1995 Champions League winner.
(Richiardi)

Center: Denmark's Peter Schmeichel, 1992 European Championship winner.
Left: Andoni Zubizaretta, World Cup '94 and Euro '96 quarter-finalist.
(Shaun Botterill and Clive Brunskill, Allsport)

Keller says the biggest difference between U. S. and English training sessions is not necessarily the content, but the purpose. "In England, there is less emphasis on practice," says Keller. "You train to stay sharp. What matters most is how you play in the game. My coach could care less if I let in goal after goal in training as long as I do my job on game day."

"I've also seen in the U. S. where a coach will have a team do an hour-and-a-half of pattern play, and everyone is falling asleep," he says. "In England, you play five-a-side and go in."

Keller does not necessarily think the American method in this respect is a bad thing. "Matter of fact, the English players could benefit from a little more structure," he observes from a position of experience.

Fan control is another place where the English could learn from America—a particularly acute issue for goalies, who spend much of their time unprotected in front of very hostile crowds. A lot has been written on English soccer violence over the years, but very few people have experienced the the Den from a goalkeeper's perspective. Millwall's notorious supporters are considered to be the rowdiest in England, and at one time the club was a bastion for hooliganism, the scourge that threatened the English game in the 1980s, but has been controlled in the 1990s.

Now the Millwall fans are known to fight, taunt, swear, spit, throw, and even chase. . .play-

Top: Norway's Erik Thorstvedt
(Richiardi)

Center: Keller's USA counterpart, U.C.L.A. graduate and Columbus Crew's Brad Freidel.
(J. B. Whitesell, ISI)

Right: Scotland's Jim Leighton; the 1998 World Cup is his fourth appearance in the finals.
(Phil Cole, Allsport)

ers that is. One time, forward Stan Collymore, then playing for Nottingham Forest, came in late on Keller, clearly intending to collide with him, or at least so it seemed to one fan in the Den. "The fan came out of the stands and chased him around for a while," recalls Keller.

"Soccer and sports in general are far more tribal in England than in the U. S.," Keller says. "In England and the rest of the world the fans become so involved. It becomes a matter of life or death to them. For me, as an American, it was hard to understand. Sports in the United States are more for enjoyment."

The press, too, has its unique angles. Keller remembers one story which was published just prior to a cup game vs. Arsenal. "It was a huge game for us and I was playing very well at the time," recalls Keller, who talked soccer with the reporter for nearly an hour. "Inside this long interview was a 30–second question about how I enjoyed fishing and hunting and when I go to Alaska I usually bring a gun just in case I run into a bear."

The next day, in gigantic block letters, the headline in *The Sun* read: "KELLER HAS MAGNUM TO FEND OFF GRIZZLIES!"

Keller says that the pressures placed on young players in England by their parents is just as bad, if not worse than the U. S. "They have Man of the Match voting for under-10s," says Keller. "Kids are worried about how many goals or how many clean sheets they have. They lose the sense that it is a team sport." At every level, what is most important to this man who earns his living in midair is that he keeps life in balance. "I saw a cartoon in *Family Circle* where little kids are watching a professional game in England," says Keller. "One of the kids asks the other, 'How come these guys play so well?' The other replied, ''Cuz their parents aren't yelling at them from the sidelines.'"

"I don't know how many caps I have, or shutouts; all I care about is winning," says Keller. "I'll concede five goals in a game if it guarantees we get six."

Winning 'keepers!
In the 1997 Tournoi de France, France's Fabien
Barthez shows England's Ian Wright
who's best with the head.
(J. B. Whitesell, ISI)

Denmark's Peter Schmeichel
blocks an Irish attack in a
1993 World Cup qualifying game.
(Dave Cannon, Allsport)

104

Germany's Andreas Koepke, Euro '96 winner, climbs above the Dutch threat, in a 1996 encounter between the two intense rivals.

(Bongarts, Richiardi)

Brazil's Claudio Taffarel, 1994 World Cup winner, is a head above France's Ibrahim Ba, in the 1997 Tournoi de France.

(J. B. Whitesell, ISI)

YANKS OVERSEAS

Before there was MLS, Yanks went to Europe. . .

Above left: Cobi Jones teamed up with Roy Wegerle in Coventry City's attack for the 1994–95 season.
(Popperfoto)

Above right: Claudio Reyna in acton for VfL Wolfsburg in a 1997 Bundesliga game vs. Bayern Munich.
(Bongarts, Richiardi)

Center: Eric Wynalda learned his professional craft with Bochum and Saarbrücken in Germany.
(Ben Radford, Allsport)

Top right: South African-born and U.S.–educated Roy Wegerle's career in England include stretches with several clubs, notably Q. P. R., Coventry City, and Blackburn Rovers in the early 1990s.
(Mike Hewitt, Allsport)

Far right: In 1993 for Sheffield Wednesday, John Harkes became the first American to play in a Wembley F. A. Cup Final; he also played for West Ham United and Derby County.
(Bob Thomas, Popperfoto)

Bottom right: Alexi Lalas (in white), defending for Padova in 1994, was the first American to play in Italy's Serie A.
(Richiardi)

CONTROLLING THE GAME
WITH CLAUDIO REYNA

They say soccer is like chess on grass. A thinking man's game. If so, then Claudio Reyna, the U. S. national team's creative central midfielder, is the queen piece, able to control the game with every single move.

His position, known traditionally as the "number 10," or linkman, can be compared to American football's quarterback, baseball's pitcher, or basketball's point guard—the player who controls the tempo of the game. The only difference is that Reyna's position is the most cerebral and improvisational in team sports. He is forced to think and create on his feet and on his own.

Unlike other sports, soccer virtually eliminates the coaches' persuasion after the whistle is blown. "It's a game where the player has to make all the decisions," says Reyna. "In other sports you can turn to your coach when you need help. I don't have the luxury of calling time-outs when I'm playing bad."

In the National Football League, there is at least one coach for every position on the field. Nearly every play starts with a coach sending a message ino the huddle. In baseball, managers look like a human windmill in the dugout, signaling to the pitcher, catcher, and other fielders what to do on every pitch. In the National Basketball Association, each coach is allowed to call up to nine time-outs in a 60-minute game.

Reyna's attraction to the thinking man's game stems from his upbringing. The son of an Argentine father and Portuguese mother, he was born with soccer in his blood. His childhood idol was Argentina's most famous number 10—Diego Maradona, a player who controlled by skill, by the power of surprise, and some-

From flying high to grounding the ball, Reyna takes responsibility for the USA's World Cup qualifying efforts in 1997. Left: Dueling with Costa Rica's Dager Villalobos. Right: Keeping Jamaica's Theodore Whitemore in check, assisted by John Harkes.

(Left: J. B. Whitesell, ISI; Right: Doug Pensinger, Allsport)

times just by reputation, the games he played in; a player always capable of extreme danger, with one incisive pass.

"My family is from Argentina so I was bred watching this kind of soccer," says Reyna, who lived for two months in Argentina when he was 12, the pivotal turning point in the development of his interest in the game. "It was fun for me to see the Brazilians and Argentines play the game with a lot of skill and flair. So I would try to play like those players. My father always preached skill and having good ball control." For the two months in Argentina, Reyna played soccer in the streets every day. "Every day," he says. "There was never a question whether you were going to play soccer. That helped."

It was never a question that Reyna was going to make it big, just how big. He dominated high school soccer at St. Benedict's Prep in New Jersey. He was *Parade* National Player of the Year twice, 1989 and 1990, and his team had a 47-game win streak, including two New Jersey state titles. He then dominated collegiate soccer during a three-time NCAA-championship career at the University of Virginia. He is now considered to be one of the most creative, skillful, and fluid players in U.S. national team history. By the time he hits his quarter-century, he will have participated in two World Cups and two Olympics, in the most demanding position.

Every time I step onto the field I must create," says Reyna, who is the starting central midfielder for VfL Wolfsburg, in the German Bundesliga (having been transferred from Bayer Leverkusen, for whom he played from 1994 to 1997). "I must get the ball to everyone. I'm the one who gets goal-scoring opportunities and the one who must set up others for opportunities." The Bundesliga has been the crucible for such brilliant playmakers as Franz Beckenbauer (from an even deeper-lying, sweeper position than Reyna plays) and Lothar Matthäus, the master of the long pass to a forward who's isolated a defender—not to forget the United States' own Thomas Dooley. But unlike Dooley, who now moves forward from a sweeper position, or USA captain John Harkes, who usually plays in close support of the forwards, Reyna's responsibility is to cover the whole field, winning the ball through rugged tackling, taking it on in tough situations, and always keeping it moving through midfield at the pace he wants his team to play—depending on the opposition, the score, and the game conditions. Argentina's Diego Simeone, Brazil's Leonardo and Roberto Carlos, England's Paul

Ince, France's Didier Deschamps and Marcel Desailly, and Romania's Georghe Hagi are the present masters of this art.

"And of course," says Reyna, "when you're at center midfield you have to defend. You can't get away with not defending." U. S. head coach Steve Sampson believes the German Bundesliga has made Reyna a more complete player. "He is not only forced to create in Germany, but also to defend," says Sampson. "His defensive work rate has improved tremendously in a short time."

Indeed, the best midfield players always pop up to make surprisingly key plays on defense when their team is being outmaneuvered. Crucial to every team's efforts to retain control of the game is possession, as once the ball is given away at this level of play, it can be very hard to recover.

Perhaps Reyna's best attribute, is the very competitive outlook he has

on his number 10 position. In the great tradition of the playmaker, which originated with inside forwards, Reyna knows, "you have to take it upon yourself to always be dangerous, to always make sure you're a threat. You have to make sure that the defender on the other team is worrying about you. He's going to have to be careful with you because in one way or another you will be the one to set up a play or get the ball moving in the right direction to set up a goal."

Here his approach is in keeping with the dangerous men of soccer, such current players as Colombia's Carlos Valderrama, Italy's Gianfranco Zola, Germany's Andreas Möller, Holland's Denis Bergkamp, France's Zinedine Zidane, Belgium's Franky Van der Elst, and England's Paul Gascoigne, all players who keep the opposition on edge because they love to burst out of midfield to make that critical pass or, even

better, to score themselves. Reyna has started to score regularly for VfL Wolfsburg, a powerful addition to his growing portfolio of attributes.

The many roles of the midfielder are illustrated by Reyna's USA teammates—a midfield fortified by experienced players all capable of defending and of scoring. From 1997 World Cup matches:

Top left: Preki Radosavljevic tangles with Jamaica's Whitemore.
(Jamie Squire, Allsport)

Center left: Thomas Dooley holds off Mexico's Luis Hernández.
Bottom left: John Harkes outruns Jamaica's Steve Malcolm.
Above: Cobi Jones breaks away from Costa Rica's Jeaustin Campos.
Above right: Joe-Max Moore slots one past Guatemala's Edgar Estrada.
Far right: Mike Sorber tussles with his Israeli counterparts.
(All photos: J. B. Whitesell, ISI)

No opposing defense has worried more about Reyna than the Mexicans did in the 1995 U. S. Cup match, in Washington, D. C., where the Americans trounced their rivals to the south 4–0. It was the most destructive defeat of Mexico in the 61-year history of this American rivalry, a performance largely due to Reyna's ability to speed up and slow down the play in the midfield. Reyna's career day ended with one goal, two assists, and one MVP trophy. "The greatest thing about my position is that you usually have the ball," Reyna says. "You have control of the game at that moment. If you're losing 1–0, you have to pick up the tempo and make things happen. If you're winning, you can slow it down and make the other team try to take it away from you." ⚽

In the midfield trenches:

Above: Brazil's Leonardo probes England's penalty area in the 1997 Tournoi de France.
(Franck Seguin, Richiardi)

Center: Argentina's captain Diego Simeone fends off an Ecuador challenge.
(Pascal Rondeau, Allsport)

Right: France's Zinedine Zidane is caught by Italy's Roberto Di Matteo in the '97 Tournoi de France.
(Ben Radford, Allsport)

Above: In the 1997 Tournoi de France, the host's Marcel Desailly out-jumps Italy's Angelo di Livio; Right: Two veterans of international combat, England's Paul Gascoigne and Germany's Stefan Kuntz collide in Euro '96 action.

(Above: J. B. Whitesell, ISI; Right: Bongarts, Richiardi)

Below: In the cauldron that is a Real Madrid vs. Barcelona match, Real's and Holland's Clarence Seedorf weighs his options against Barca's and Nigeria's Emanuel Amunike.

(Ben Radford, Allsport)

WEARING THE NUMBER 10 SHIRT

It was the number that Pelé wore, that Maradona wore, that all the inside forwards of yesteryear became heroes with. In days past, when substitutions were limited to one reserve (who always wore 12), a number belonged to a position not a player. In this day of squads, with each player assigned a number for the entire season, as in American pro sports, the number 10 has become a little less revered but is still often worn by the player whose playing personality can dictate his team's style. As more complicated tactical formations have been employed in soccer this de-cade—as teams have changed from 4–3–3 or 4–4–2 to combinations of deep-lying, playmaking forwards plus attacking midfielders sup-porting them—a formation might now be something like 3–2–3–2—versatility is required of most players; but even in the most balanced teams there still tends to be a player who carries the burden of blending the midfield into an attacking shape—and through him the game travels. ⚽

Left: Holland's Denis Bergkamp, seen scoring for his club Arsenal against Kasey Keller and Leicester City, is perhaps today's quintessential inside forward and playmaker.
(Left: Mark Thompson, Allsport)

Above left: Bulgaria's Krassimir Balakov (with France's Christian Karembeu) helped take a nation that had never won a World Cup finals game to the 1994 semifinal and to Euro '96 and France '98 qualification. Above right: Thomas Hässler took Germany to the 1994 World Cup quarterfinals and the 1996 European championship.
(Above and above right: Richiardi)

DEFENDING YOUR TURF
WITH EDDIE POPE

In 1995, Eddie Pope's biggest concern on the soccer field was marking teenage forwards from arch rival University of South Carolina. One year later, he was in charge of shutting down some of the most deadly goal scorers in the world, including Argentina's and Parma's Hernan Crespo, Costa Rica's and Derby County's Paulo Wanchope, and Nigeria's Olympic gold medalist Daniel Amokachi.

When Pope was 21 he was a college kid studying political science at the University of North Carolina. When he was 22, he was a national team starter and professional soccer player, scoring the winning goal (a header off a free kick) for D. C. United in the inaugural MLS Cup final—a golden goal at that, as sudden death was used to settle the tie with the L. A. Galaxy. He also went from playing in front of 1,000 fans at Chapel Hill to playing in front of 80,000 crazed, flag-waving Americans in Birmingham, Alabama, at the 1996 Olympics.

In that short period of time, Pope became perhaps the country's best one-on-one defender. He is quick, he is strong, he is smart, and he is a threat to come forward and score on set pieces. The 1997 Major League Soccer defender of the

Left: Going for the ball, despite the man, USA's Eddie Pope outplays Costa Rica's Ronald Gomez in the 1997 World Cup qualifying game.
(Shaun Botterill, Allsport)

Above: The USA–Mexico rivalry has become an intense clash of wills for CONCACAF superiority and World Cup qualification. After losing at home to Mexico and striker Zaque, Pope and his fellow defenders led the short-handed USA to a memorable 0–0 shutout in Mexico City's Azteca Stadium.
(J. B. Whitesell, ISI)

year is expected to be the backbone of the USA defense for years to come.

So what's it like having the assignment of marking the opposition's top goal scorer during a World Cup qualifier? Pope says it can be intimidating (you would never notice by watching him), you must have good positioning or you'll get burned, and you can't be distracted by the head games. "It can be nerve-wracking," says Pope. "And, yes, I do still get nervous. I think it is good. I like to be nervous because it makes me more alert. If you're too relaxed I think you can get complacent and that's not good."

Nerves were at an all-time high in his first full international match. Pope is among a handful of players in the 84-year formal history of the U.S. national team who have made their international debut in the pressured environment of a World Cup qualifier. Most players get the luxury of starting their national team careers with an international friendly match—a game which means relatively little. He debuted as a starter against Trinidad and Tobago in the USA's second World Cup qualifier for France '98. "I just remember thinking back then [against Trinidad] that you may only get one chance to prove yourself to the coach," Pope recalls.

And prove himself, he did. The U. S. won 2–0. Trinidad and Tobago's exceptionally speedy front-runner, Dwight Yorke, regularly among the goal-scoring leaders in the English Premier League (he plays for Aston Villa), did not score, and so the lanky, soft-spoken Pope had taken advantage of his one chance by solidifying his position in the back line.

Ask Pope how he marks forwards and he will tell you like it is an exact science. "It's all about good positioning, getting goal side of the ball, so they don't get in behind you with one pass," Pope says.

"I keep an eye on the ball and an eye on the forward. The key is to mark very tight in the box and make sure they don't get that extra yard off you, where they can get that opportunity to finish," he says.

Watch Pope on the field and you'll notice he rarely gives his forward an opportunity to touch the ball, let alone a chance to score.

He learned it's all about anticipation and positioning; not letting the forward get away from him—or get sight of the goal. Good

Above: Holding off his man, long-time USA veteran Jeff Agoos repels Mexico's Carlos Hermosillo.
Left: Consummate defender, England's Tony Adams out-leans Scotland's Gordon Durie in Euro '96 action.
(Above: J. B. Whitesell, ISI; left: Richiardi)

defenders aren't afraid to play right next to their man, no matter his speed or strength.

"The best way to make sure a forward doesn't beat you is to not let him get the ball," he says. "If you're marking tight enough, he'll be forced to play the ball backwards. The last thing you want is a guy like Mexico's Zaque getting the ball, being able to turn and run at you," Pope says. "That's when things get difficult."

At the tender age of 23 you would think Pope would be prime bait for a psych job—forwards trying to beat him mentally rather than physically. Forwards telling him how they are going to beat him all day long (unfortunately trash talking is part of international soccer, too).

Getting a reaction out of Eddie Pope in a game is like trying to squeeze lemon juice out of an orange. . . . It can't be done. "I never talk to forwards," Pope says, "no matter what they say. If they say something I just ignore them."

He has a much better way of dealing with the all too eccentric goal-scoring types. "The best way to get inside a forward's head is to shut them out for the first 45–50 minutes," he says. "If you can do this, they are usually out of the game. They haven't had their chances and they're frustrated."

Playing for D. C. United and the national

World Cup and Olympic Games veteran Mike Burns shows the USA's defensive resolve in a U. S. Cup '97 match vs. Peru.
(J. B. Whitesell, ISI)

team has meant Pope has had to face a wide variety of playing styles, from the speedy, short-passing, crafty up-the middle play of Tampa Bay Mutiny or the Mexican national team to the counterattacking style of Costa Rica to the rugged aerial game preferred by Jamaica.

He ranks the hardest forwards he has had to shut down as Paulo Wanchope, Eduardo Hurtado, and fellow teammates Jaime Moreno (D. C. United) and Roy Lassiter (USA).

After the mind game, there is the physical game. As Pope says, "A player like Paulo Wanchope is difficult to mark because he is physically dominant. He's big, strong, has a good touch and he's crafty. Eduardo Hurtado [Los Angeles Galaxy and Ecuador] is similar to Wanchope, but less crafty. Even though you know where he's going most of the time, he is still difficult because of his brute strength."

Spanish, British, Scandinavian, and German defenders, particularly, are well-versed in matching forwards with power. But Pope knows, from marking Bolivian international Moreno in training, that sheer speed and technique equal to those of the quickest forwards—perhaps best exemplified in the defensive play of such stars as Italy's Paolo Maldini, France's Lilian Thuram, Holland's Ronald de Boer, and Brazil's Aldair—are essential components of an international defender's game now.

Then there is sheer effort: "Roy Lassiter only needs a little window of opportunity to score and he tries all game long, for 90 minutes. I've never had trouble marking him but the fact is it is a pain in the butt to mark him for 90 minutes because he does not stop trying. Where with a lot of other forwards, if you shut them down for the first half, you've seen all their moves, so their game is over."

Making sure an attacker's game is over is Pope's principle purpose. But the best defense can be a good attack, and while not a sweeper, carrying the ball upfield and threatening on the breakaway, in the mold of Borussia Dortmund's and Germany's Matthias Sammer, Pope moves forward to assist in the air on set pieces, like many a classic center-half, including national teammates Marcelo Balboa and Alexi Lalas.

From just such a position, he scored that golden goal that decided the MLS inaugural championship–and developed his thirst for more victories and further goals.

So where does Pope go from here? He is years from hitting his prime and has accomplished so much. "You can never win enough," says Pope, talking like he expects many more championship rings. "It's infectious. But most of all I want to satisfy myself and be able to say that I played well in this game or this season, helping my team win."

Then he adds with reasoned balance: "Once your soccer falls into place everything else will follow." ⚽

Germany's Matthias Sammer is a sweeper who attacks in the Beckenbauer mold and threatens often to score.
(TempSport, Richiardi)

Italy's Paolo Maldini defends in style and often attacks down the wing; the 1994 World Cup finalist's father coached the Italian national team to the 1998 World Cup.
(JMD, Popperfoto)

France's Lilian Thuram, Christian Karembeu, and Laurent Blanc crowd out Holland's de Kock in Euro '96 action.
(CMO, Popperfoto)

Ever-battling, Wynalda is the USA's target man—winning the ball and winning games. In World Cup '98 qualifying action against Mexico's Pavel Pardo (left), Trinidad and Tobago's Marvin Faustin (above) and Mexico's Duilio Davino (right).

(All photos: J. B. Whitesell, ISI)

GOAL SCORING
WITH ERIC WYNALDA

Go deep inside the mind of the U.S. National Team's all-time leading scorer and you'll find that he has all the qualities of a great striker. He's confident, he's brash, he's emotional, he idolizes someone, and he dreams every night. But ask Wynalda what makes him tick and he says it is none of the above. "My biggest strength is that I don't beat myself," he says. "I have always been able to beat people different ways. I have always been able to score with my head or equally well with both feet, but more recently in my career I don't beat myself when it comes to a big chance."

Wynalda has capitalized on some of the biggest chances. His goal against Switzerland in the United States's opening game in the 1994 World Cup, a curving 25-yard direct free kick into the upper left corner, is perhaps his most well-known strike. The first goal in Major League Soccer, an individual effort from the left side which won Goal of the Year honors in 1996, is Wynalda's most historic goal. In terms of international matches, Wynalda is the USA's most prolific goal scorer in history. His goal total donning the red, white, and blue strip is more than double the next active U.S. player. And he is, without a doubt, the biggest threat in the U.S. arsenal. "When I have an opportunity to score a goal I stick to what I know," Wynalda says. "I don't think too much; I'll let what comes naturally happen. That's what my strength is and usually my instincts are right. It has taken me a long time to get there. I don't have a set move or a set shot, I just beat the goalkeeper. That's it."

Wynalda overflows with confidence: ask him his weaknesses and he will tell you, but not until after a long pondering pause. "I don't take advantage of the dive enough and I could be better in the air," he eventually mutters. He says that he is blessed with a very good soccer body but others say it is his confident mind that makes him what he is. "I have the mentality of trusting myself," he says. "I take a lot of pride in that I don't panic in front of the net. Younger players or inexperienced players who don't take it to the next level have a tendency to make plays in front of the goal, the simple situations, more dramatic in their mind. I don't. It's psychological."

He's brash, too: many players have tried, unsuccessfully, to get inside the mind of Wynalda while defending him. They try to disrupt his equilibrium. "I have been the victim of more psych jobs," Wynalda says. It usually starts with a conversation about broken bones and ends with a catchy in-your-face comment from Wynalda. "They say they are going to break my leg and I say please go for the right one because the left has already been broken once. I'm not scared of anything much now. It used to scare me. Do you think he really means that?" When somebody talks to him, Wynalda thrives on acting like nothing gets to him. "I put those thoughts away. I don't make it personal any-more," says the player who used to be a regular yellow and—some-

times red card re-cipient. "After I've scored two goals and we're up 2–0 in the 88th minute and we're pret-ty much going to win. Then, if some-body says something, I'll come from behind and whisper in their ear. 'You can take that one to the bank.' Or I'll say 'I will see you next time but the way you performed tonight you may never play again.'"

In one German Bundesliga match, Wynalda, playing then for FC Saarbrücken (he later played for VfL Bochum), got an 1860 Munich player thrown out of the game for physically retaliating after one of Wynalda's brash statements. "In fact he was so mad he started chasing me all over the field," re-calls Wynalda, who scored 9 goals in his first 10 games that year. "I don't think he liked Americans. He was upset that an American could come over to his country and do well."

He's emotional: with 13 minutes left to be played in a

scoreless battle between the United States and Costa Rica in front of a sold out Civic Stadium in Portland, Oregon, U. S. midfielder Tab Ramos scored one of the most important, not to mention beautiful, goals in U.S. soccer history, giving the Americans a crucial 1–0 victory. It was Ramos' first World Cup qualifier since recovering from a grueling seven-month rehabilitation process for a torn anterior cruciate ligament. Wynalda sat on the bench that day. He had pulled up in warm-ups with a badly strained calf muscle. He could not play. He could barely walk. "When Tab scored I jumped up and tried to chase him, I was so happy," remembers Wynalda. "When I realized I couldn't run, I started crying. I then hobbled over to the corner of the field and cried. I was a mess. I was totally, totally crying," he says.

He idolizes someone: "Wayne Gretzky is my ultimate idol," Wynalda said. "He plays his game with the ultimate finesse and speed. There is something about him that is very special. He is very cocky but you would never know it. There is no athlete in the world who has dominated his sport more." Wynalda sees a lot of similarities between the two. "He makes the right decision when he has the puck and he always gets more assists than goals. If I have an opportunity to shoot, I'll shoot. But if it's 80 percent I'm going to score and 100 percent that someone else is going to score, they are going to get the ball. That's the way I have always played it. Gretzky does that." "My ultimate dream is to play golf with him," says Wynalda. "Have the opportunity to talk with him. See what goes on in his head. What is it like to be called 'The Great One?'"

He dreams every night: "I don't think there is a night I don't

You never tire of seeing the ball hit the net, said Bundesliga and English icon Kevin Keegan about the great strikers: England's Teddy Sheringham (10) watches an Alan Shearer (seated) shot sail past the Swiss goalkeeper in Euro '96.
(Mike Hewitt, Allsport)

One of the world's most decorated forwards, national team captain Jürgen Klinsmann opens the scoring for Germany against Armenia in a 4–0 World Cup '98 qualifying match. A fluent master of the art, Klinsmann has starred for clubs in Germany (twice), Italy (twice), France, and England (twice).

(Bongarts, Richiardi)

dream about something I want to do," says Wynalda. "The other night I had a pretty vivid one." The setting was a soccer field and Wynalda was dreaming that he was playing against Costa Rica and was just about ready to take a direct free kick. "I remember seeing all the faces in the wall," he recalls. "I looked down at the ball and then looked up and everything had changed. All the faces were different and we were playing Italy in the World Cup in France. I hit the free kick, it hit the crossbar, bounced down, beat the goalkeeper and John Harkes did a diving header. The next thing I know we were all inside the net celebrating a goal which ended up to be the winning goal in the World Cup Final. It was a great dream. I woke up almost crying."

Wynalda's dream is shared, of course, as you would expect by all the world's strikers. "The game is about glory, doing things in style," wrote the highly decorated Northern Irish player and commentator Danny Blanchflower, a concept often echoed in the soccer world and usually meaning overwhelming the opposition with goals. In the early 1990s, fundamental suggestions were made to improve scoring (such as increasing the size of the goal), but the 1994 World Cup reversed the downward trend and there now seems to be no lack of goals—or goal scorers. 1916 goals were scored in the 643 World Cup France qualifying matches, including a record 17–0 Iran defeat of the Maldives. By continental zone, Iran's Bagheri (18 goals), Mexico's Hermosillo (10), Yugoslavia's Mijatovic and Milosevic (14 and 10), South Africa's Masinga (9), and Chile's Zamorano and Salas (12 and 11) led the 1997 qualifying onslaught.

Teams are now flush with strikers, from young stars, such as Spain's Raul, Italy's Vieri and del Piero, and Nigeria's Amokachi to such veterans as England's Shearer, Sheringham, and Wright, Colombia's Asprilla, and Belgium's Van der Elst (making his fourth consecutive appearance in the World Cup finals). In Europe, attacking soccer is back. Even in Serie A (if not in Italy's national team play), the legacy of Herrera's catenaccio is under threat from such prolific scorers as Holland's Kluivert, Argentina's Batistuta and Crespo, France's Zidane, Germany's Bierhoff, and, of course, Ronaldo, Brazil's superstar.

The U.S. national team also has a corps of strikers to support Eric Wynalda up front: Roy Lassiter, Brian McBride, and Preki Radosavljevic have had league-leading performances in MLS play; Roy Wegerle has a veteran's developed eye for the net, while Jovan Kirovski, who learned his trade in the reserves at Manchester United and then Borussia Dortmund, scored in the Champions League and became the first American to play in the Intercontinental Club Championship, when Borussia beat Brazil's Cruzeiro, 2–0, late in 1997. The future bodes well for the confident, the brash, the emotional, the dreamers. . .the goal scorers. ⚽

ROMÁRIO AND RONALDO

"Ronaldo. Romário.' 'Romário. Ronaldo.' Either way it rolls off the tongue and either way it has become a mantra from Porto Alegre in the south to Rio de Janeiro and Belem further north. Exactly one year before they begin defending their World Cup title," wrote Christopher Clarey in a profile of the duo in *The New York Times* in the summer of 1997, "the Brazilians again appear to possess the most dangerous striker tandem in international soccer. In the United States in 1994, Bebeto was Romário's sidekick, and even though the team that backed them up was busier defending than channeling the bulk of its energy into offensive artistry, the two strikers' individual talents were decisive. Ronaldo, then 17, watched every memorable minute from the bench. 'It was difficult not to play,' he said. 'But I learned a lot

from
Romário
and Bebeto.
They were on top
of their games.' "
When the duo imperiously
punched in 3 goals apiece in Brazil's
6–0 obliteration of a strong Australia side in
the 1997 Confederations Cup Final, a competition
between continental federations champions held in Saudi
Arabia, they appeared every bit as unstoppable and legendary as the siroccos that sweep over desert sands.
Romário de Souza Farias and his counterpart, Ronaldo Luiz
Nazario de Lima, almost ten years his junior, were simply
repeating the quality of performance they had begun to
demonstrate almost as flawlessly in the Tournoi de France
six months earlier.

It is that rarest of combinations: a striking partnership of
unique fluidity created by two players known for their audacious individuality. As they spearhead a team that seems
intent on dominating opponents in every department, a
team that clearly has all the attacking intentions of their
1958 and 1970 predecessors and the defensive measure of
their 1994 championship squad, they have unusual freedom
to execute their remarkable pas de deux as they please.

Destiny has been kind: the crafty veteran Romário, moving

*Left: Romário rounds Italy's goalkeeper to score in the 1997 Tournoi
de France. Center: Brazil's strike force share passes, goals, and glory.
Above: Ronaldo sidesteps Paraguay's Carlos Gamarra in the 1997
Copa America.*

(Left and above: Allsport. Center: Richiardi)

toward the twilight of a career that brought him FIFA footballer of the year in 1994 (and runner-up in 1993), was thoroughly rejuvenated by the arrival of the fully matured Ronaldo, who won the award in 1996 and 1997. Indeed, "Ronaldomania," the soccer world's coronation of the center forward as the sport's greatest active star, seemed to make Brazil's national team players unusually determined to excel as a unified squad—shaving their heads en masse, for example, for the Confederations Cup tournament.

Ronaldo is accompanied by an outstanding crop of young players, including the formidable Denilson. And with A. C. Milan's veteran Leonardo and Real Madrid's Roberto Carlos also bringing exceptional power to bear, a secure defense anchored by the 1994 stars Aldair and goalkeeper Claudio Taffarel, and coach Mario Zagallo as the unabashed link to the glorious past, comparisons with Brazil's legendary teams were frequent in the buildup to the 1998 tournament.

Ronaldo and Romário "share the same home city (Rio de Janeiro), the same very modest economic backgrounds, and the same ability to go from first to fourth gear in a big hurry," Christopher Clarey continued. "Both have led the Brazilian, Dutch, and Spanish leagues in scoring. Like Romário, Ronaldo left Brazil for

Taking on the Paris Saint-Germain defense in his last game for Barcelona, the 1997 European Cup Winner's Cup Final. Ronaldo won the cup for the Spanish club with a penalty.

(Ben Radford, Allsport)

P.S.V. Eindhoven in Holland; like Romário he was then sold to Spain's high-profile Barcelona, where he promptly became the role model of choice on playgrounds around the world by ramming home spectacular goal after spectacular goal."

They have almost identical lineages. Both began at small clubs: Romário at Orlario, Ronaldo at São Cristavao (where he was coached by 1970 star winger Jairzinho). Both then moved to big clubs, Cruzeiro for Ronaldo, Vasco da Gama for Romário, before moving to Holland's P.S.V. Eindhoven. Both have had several utterly remarkable purple patches: Ronaldo, for example, scored 54 goals in his first 54 games for Cruzeiro; Romário's resume includes 67 goals in his first 69 games for Eindhoven and a hat-trick on his debut for Barca. Both played at critical moments in their development for former English national team coach Bobby Robson—and both could bridle sometimes at his tactics. Like Romário, who left Barcelona in December 1994 after two "tempestuous seasons" for Flamengo (then back to Spain and Valencia, and back to Flamengo again), Ronaldo's Spanish career also finished acrimoniously when he left Barca for Italy's Internazionale amidst a bitter contract and transfer-fee dispute that required FIFA intervention to resolve.

Both players are also brilliant, courageous dribblers of the ball who employ trademark high-speed surges to get them straight through massed ranks of defenders. Both excel at tying defenders into knots at close quarters, but the impressively muscled Ronaldo has the edge in this department over any forward in memory, for "when opponents try to shove, hack, or bump him off course," which is usually their only resort, "he does not tumble melodramatically into a writhing heap in hope of hearing a referee's whistle. Ronaldo bumps back and dribbles on. . . .'The compliments he is receiving are not exaggerated,' Pelé has said."

Facing Serie A's famed *catenaccio* defenses, Ronaldo has simply reinforced his status as the world's number 1. Unlike Romário, who has found himself unsettled at most of his clubs and consequently courted his share of controversial notoriety, Ronaldo, for all his burdens of fame, is apparently unusually unaffected by pressure or temptations. He explained to *France Football* that he most admires such players as Zico and Pelé, whose stellar comportment off the field has matched their excellence on it. And he told Christopher Clarey, "We are all playing with the same goal: winning games. I like it that way. No star, everybody the same."

While he also told *France Football* at the end of 1997 that he longed for "a little month" off from his packed club and international program of matches, his and Romário's immutable date with the 1998 World Cup tournament seemed more a matter of destiny than schedule. As Hugh McIlvanney once observed about the supreme showmanship and gifted excellence of Brazil's international players, "They believed their football was made for World Cup finals and couldn't wait to prove it." ⚽

Mexico's star forward Luis Hernández tangles with
Ecuadoran defender Luis Capurro in the 1997 Copa
America.

(Allsport)

Italy's striker and winger Alessandro Del Piero finds himself blocked
by Russia's Vladislav Rasimov in Euro '96.

(Shaun Botterill)

Inter's Ivan Zamorano was pivotal in Chile's soaring to the 1998 World Cup finals.
(Richiardi)

Holland's and Milan's Patrick Kluivert keeps out of trouble against Yugoslavia's and Lazio's Jugovic in 1997 Serie A action.
(Richiardi)

Headed for a "Batigol": Argentina's and
Fiorentina's famed scorer Gabriel Batistuta
tests the highly decorated (scudetto and
Intercontinental Cup winners) Juventus
wall in 1997 Serie A action.

(Richiardi)

*With the speed and verve that is Brazilian, Monaco's and Brazil's
Sonny Anderson (now with Barcelona) rockets a goal past the
Newcastle defense in 1997 UEFA Cup action.*

(Stu Forster, Allsport)

CELEBRATION!

Perhaps the most enduring look of World Cup '94: Luis Enrique celebrates
a goal for Spain against Switzerland.
(Simon Bruty, Allsport)

Spain's Kiko and Raul locked in Euro '96 joy, vs. Bulgaria.
(Richiardi)

After stealing the Euro '96 match from
Scotland with a superb solo goal,
England's star of the '90s
Paul Gascoigne gets
soaked himself.
(Popperfoto)

"Love is good for footballers—as long as it's not at halftime," said Richard Moller Nielson, Denmark's coach—but it can be exhausting mid-match. Borussia Dortmund celebrate during their 1997 European Champions League 3–1 triumph over Juventus.

(Bongarts, Richiardi)

His very own fashion statement, Champions League winner in 1996 with Juventus, F. A. Cup winner in 1997 with Chelsea; Italy's Gianluca Vialli sends a souvenir to the fans, vs. Sampdoria.

(Richiardi)

1996 MLS defender of the
year John Doyle celebrates a
goal for the San Jose Clash.

(John Todd, MLS/Allsport)

Turning the soccer world upside down: Celestine Barbayaro, after Nigeria's first goal in the 3–2 Olympic gold-medal triumph over Argentina.
(Bob Thomas, Popperfoto)

A familiar look: Germany celebrates yet another triumph, this time vs. Russia in Euro '96. As Simon Evans has written, "When it comes to the ultimate test of a nation's footballing ability, the Germans deliver."

(Richiardi)

Carin Gabarra (12) and Joy Fawcett lead
the parade, as the U. S. women celebrate
their 1994 Olympic gold-medal victory, over
China, 2–1, in Athens, Georgia.

(Bob Thomas, Popperfoto)

Right: With
goalposts, if not
goals to size, America's girls
most often find their first team experience is in
playing soccer. Above: The most dominant collegiate
dynasty, celebrating their 1997 NCAA triumph: the
University of North Carolina has an extraordinary 415–16–11
record and 15 national championships since 1980.
(Both photos: J. B. Whitesell, ISI)

From one generation to the next: Joy Fawcett, mother of two,
regular starter, and one of the best defenders in the world, accepts
the accolades after a 1997 international vs. South Korea.
(Allsport)

WOMEN'S SOCCER
MARIANNE BHONSLAY

important historic event than the announcement of Korea/Japan 2000." The 1999 Women's World Cup, Rothenberg continued, "will be what turns around women's soccer. It will be a showcase for the sport and [the U. S.] women." The expectation is that the Women's World Cup, a championship which commenced in 1991, will field 16 teams over 19 playing days: the intention is to have a collective viewing audience of one billion in 1999.

It will not, however, be the first time the U. S. women's national team will be in the spotlight. In fact, of the many adjectives employed to characterize the national team, perhaps one portrays the squad most appropriately: preeminent. In this past decade as women's soccer emerged as a significant facet in the female sports explosion, the U. S. team facilitated its ascendance and worldly preeminence with a combination of innate athleticism, disciplined coaching, and a resolute resilence often resulting in notable renaissances. Coupled with a cultural mantra now embracing women athletes and amplified investments from the USSF, the Americans are marked as the perennial elite of women's soccer. Indeed, with the winning of the inaugural Women's World Championship title in 1991 and the gold-medal in the 1996 Olympics, the U. S. ventures into the 1999 FIFA Women's World Cup tournament as a distinct favorite.

"Unlike in men's soccer [the U. S.] started its women's program at about the same time as the rest of the world," commented Rothenberg, referring to the 1980s. And with the advent of Title IX (in 1972), which instilled a massive increase of support for women's sports in American colleges, and a society "more open to [opportunities] for women than other countries," Rothenberg noted, the women's national team was able to attain world parity, indeed notoriety, early in its playing tenure.

"Our society is accepting of women as professional athletes," explains Tiffeny Milbrett, who scored the match-winning goal in the 1996 Olympic final against China that earned the U. S. the gold medal. "Most countries don't accept women athletes well. They aren't as supportive." And, Milbrett adds, "Our American athlete mentality and our physique [are advantages]." National team co-captain Carla Overbeck concurs: "We're all very athletic, we are technical and we have a tremendous amount of heart. We might not be as technical as [for example] the Chinese, but we seem more determined. You can't teach that. As Americans, we

It may have appeared to be bad luck. Simply, so to speak, an unfortunate luck of the draw. The day FIFA announced that Japan and Korea would host the 2002 World Cup, the United States was pronounced the host nation for the 1999 Women's World Cup. Once again, the men dominated the headlines. How could it not be so? Yet with typical aplomb, when U. S. Soccer president Alan Rothenberg addressed the press that day, he rather unorthodoxly proclaimed that when the soccer world reflected on FIFA's concurrent announcements in 25 or 50 years, "the granting of the Women's World Cup to the United States will be remembered as a more

have that."

U. S. National Team Coach Tony DiCicco can attest to his players' perseverance. During the United States national team bus ride to the 1995 Women's World Championship dinner in Stockholm, DiCiccio addressed his squad, which had relinquished its world title, remarking on the team's third-place finish. "The margin [of our loss] on the field was so small," DiCicco, recalls conveying to the U. S. team, referring to Norway's 1–0 win over the club in the semifinals. But at the dinner, DiCicco continued, the team would be "invisible."

Indeed, the U. S. team sat on the sidelines that night as the newly crowned Norwegians accepted the championship trophy. The difference between winning and placing third, DiCicco espoused, "is the difference between being seen and recognized and being forgotten."

DiCicco's harsh but carefully calculated words resonated with the U. S. squad. While team members were lamenting the loss of their champion status, DiCicco was nurturing the motivation necessary to regain the title. "Failure affords opportunity," explains DiCicco, who took over as the USA's head coach from Anson Dorrance in 1994. "Failure can be catastrophic, but it can also be something you can use. I used it at the championship dinner. Losing provided the motivation necessary to train and prepare to regain the title."

The first gauge in that quest was the 1996 Olympics. In a remarkable five-day period, the U. S. thwarted challenges by the Norwegians and Chinese, revenging their 1995 World Championship loss with a 2–1 overtime win over Norway in the semifinals. A 2–1 defeat of China in the Olympic final, attended by some 80,000 fans in Athens, Georgia, reaffirmed the Americans stature as a powerhouse. It also afforded the women—and U. S. Soccer—the world platform that arrives with an Olympic victory, one which engenders recognition and respect. "People outside [of athletics] can comprehend a gold medal," says Milbrett. "It doesn't matter that we're women. We're gold-medal athletes."

Yet a special stature has been a factor in the U. S. program since the mid-1980s when the foundation of this current American team was assembled. "A genetic crop of extraordinary women came along at the same time," explains University of North Carolina Coach Anson Dorrance, who presided over the team from 1986 through 1994.

That group included Overbeck and Kristine Lilly, who were 19 and 16, respectively, when they debuted with the team, and current veterans such as Michelle Akers, Joy Fawcett, Julie Foudy, Carin Jennings (now Gabarra), and Mia Hamm, who was 15 when she joined the team.

"Our core has been playing together a heck of a long time," Dorrance continues. "One of the best decisions [made] when organizing the team was to go with a group of young players before they had proven themselves. We selected a core and stuck with them. We invested in them. It's paying huge dividends now." Adds Overbeck, who played a record 63 con-

secutive games for the U. S. team, between 1993 and 1997, "Our core has been together since 1987, '88. We've grown up together. We're determined to be the best in the world." The result is a skillful, accomplished team, whose members are accustomed to playing and training with each other, yet youthful enough to retain its speed and stamina. Seven members have attained the 100-cap mark. "The core is still wonderfully young, tremendously athletic and experienced," Dorrance adds. "How do you compete with young experience?"

Not easily, as U. S. rivals will assert. Following an August 1985 tournament in Italy, in which the U. S. dropped three of four matches, the team compiled an astounding 106–25–9 record through January 1997, including the '91 World Championship and '96 Olympics gold medal.

Moreover, during this tenure, the team has embellished and refined its technical attributes. Endowed with "incredible one vs. one" talent, according to Dorrance, the Americans evolved their tactics, incorporating a "better possessional game."

The playing style of the '91 championship, Dorrance relates, was characterized by the squad's "take-on artists." Seven of eleven players were "one vs. one" prodigies, he professes, noting the deftness of Fawcett, Foudy, Hamm, Lilly, Akers, Jennings, and now national team assistant coach April Heinrichs, who captained that team. Now the team is "layering in additional strengths without losing previous strengths," Dorrance reiterates. Those supplemental techniques were fostered by DiCicco, who was with the team in '91 as an assistant coach at the championships and took over as the head coach in 1994.

"In '91 in China [the players were] fit, athletic, competitive and combative," DiCicco recounts. "Players were skilled, [they] ran hard, looked for openings." Now, he adds, players have become "smarter."

Following the '95 championships, DiCicco details, the style of play became "more deliberate," with players keeping possession to "make [the opposing team] work, chase the ball and wear them down."

In fact, DiCicco adds, he instituted a "systematically" different style of soccer. "We went from a man-to-man [with] a sweeper in the back to a zone system." Furthermore, he says, "Our system [is to] exploit the other team or to neutralize the other team." In 1995, DiCicco claims, the U. S. was not "the best team. Norway was a better team." In '96, at the Olympics, he says, "we were the better team."

And perhaps the squad with the most experience. "Our experience is a huge strength," affirms Lilly, who has been with the national team since 1985 and is headed for the eminent number of 150 caps.

Experience, Lilly further suggests, cultivates confidence. "One of our main strengths is our mentality," Lilly continues, pointing to the team's ability to play a second half with the same, or more, fortitude than the first 45 minutes. When the team traveled to Europe in the fall of '97, it played Germany twice, dropping the first match. In the rematch, the U. S. was leading 1–0, then added two goals as if to reaffirm its dominance. The gravy goals, Lilly adds pointedly, "were to kill their spirit."

The team's experience, confidence, technique and athleticism will likely be tested in coming years, specifically during its quest to regain the world title in 1999. In the early 1990s, perhaps four nations could credibly challenge for a world title. Today that field has doubled or tripled. "We don't take any team lightly," offers Kristine Lilly, who debuted with the team in 1987, scoring her first goal 10 days later in a match against China. "We respect everyone we play. It's not just the top 4 teams [that are competitive]," Lilly adds, referring to Germany, China, and Norway along with the U. S. "It's the top 10 teams." Countries such as Sweden, Denmark, Australia, Brazil—and to a lesser extent Holland and France—now possess the potential to upset the U. S. in any given match.

Consequently, while the Americans retain the enviable position of being considered a top rival of most countries, the U. S. must likewise play its best soccer each match to be assured a win. There are no "easy" matches.

Toward that end, the USSF is augmenting its support for its women's team. In early 1997, the federation signed an estimated 16 elite players to contracts through August 1999, assuring the athletes of monthly salaries, allowing them to train as "professionals" through the '99 World Cup. "The fact that [the athletes] are full-time employees for two years as we build up to the World Championships [demonstrates our] commit-

The international women's game is now contested at the top by such perennial powers as Norway, winner of the 1993 World Cup, as well as rising power Brazil, shown here (Marianne Pettersen from Norway; Formiga and Elaine from Brazil) competing for the bronze medal in the 1996 Olympic Games.

(Left: TempSport, Richiardi; Above: Popperfoto)

ment," says Tom King, general manager of U. S. Soccer's national teams. This agreement, King notes, which stipulates monthly salary requirements, allows the athletes to train "full-time" and focus on soccer as a "career."

Notes Tiffeny Milbrett, "The [Federation] has given us enough [salary] so we can have soccer as our only job." Moreover, that financial commitment, induces U.S. Soccer to seek a return on its investment, which likely portends establishing a series of very high-caliber, well-produced, and aggressively advertised international matches for the squad. "Once we committed to that kind of money, we need a return on the investment," claims Rothenberg, noting that the federation has invested as much as 5 million dollars in its women's program since 1991 and will initiate an "ambitious" schedule of games, perhaps as many as 50, for 1998 and through the first half of 1999. Given that most USA players only find they have truly competitive matches when they are playing for the national team, adding to the schedule can only improve the team. The U. S. also created a "residency" program for the women, including a facility where the athletes could live and train while

Above: Co-captain of the national team and winner of the 1997 FIFA Fair Play Award, Julie Foudy, seen here in a 1997 game vs. Germany, has been a regular starter for USA teams since 1988, when she was 17.
Right: The king of motivation, USA's Tony DiCicco is fast becoming the winningest coach in U. S. soccer history; seen here rallying the team after a 1997 1–3 loss to Germany; days later they won the rematch 3–0.
Above: Briana Scurry, the most capped goalkeeper in U. S. soccer history, celebrates the 1996 Olympic Games triumph.
(All photos: J. B. Whitesell, ISI)

preparing for major tournaments and events. The national players resided in Orlando as they prepared for the '95 World Championships and the '96 Olympics and were expecting to return to a residence either in Florida or Southern California, perhaps San Diego, in January 1999. "The residential program is the single most important thing to the evolution of the team," remarks Coach Tony DiCicco, citing the ability to monitor his players' nutrition and fitness to "maximize performance."

And optimum performance will be critical in the women's quest to regain its world title. Should that goal be attained in 1999, many believe the United States will have capped off a remarkable 15 years in women's soccer.

Says Tony DiCicco, "It's important for the United States that this team has a legacy of being the best team ever." For DiCicco that means the United States women establish preeminence, one similarly reflected by formidable [men's] teams such as the "Real Madrids of the '50s and '60s and the Brazils of the '60s and '70s, or the 1927 Yankees," says DiCicco. "Teams that stand out. Winning the World Cup in 1999 and [another gold medal] in 2000 would put a stamp on [U. S.] women's soccer that will never be duplicated." ⚽

Showing her feared acceleration, and
on her way to one of her two assists in
the 1996 Olympics final, USA's celebrated
Mia Hamm pulls away from China's Yunjie Fan.
(J. B. Whitesell, ISI)

MIA HAMM: THE WORLD'S BEST PLAYER
WITH TONY DICICCO

She debuted for the United States women's national team in 1987, as a shy 15-year old, with her eyes full of wonder, her heart overflowing with spirit, and her legs full of goals. Today, she is still the youngest player ever to don the U. S. senior team jersey. She has not only become the country's leading player, she is widely considered the world's best player. . .and more: she is the one most considered to be leading women's team sports to prominence.

Armed with incredible natural talent and an insatiable drive to win, Mariel Margaret Hamm, who learned her game astonishingly quickly in Texas schoolgirls' leagues and national youth development programs, did not set out to revolutionize women's soccer. She certainly did not dream about endorsements or fame. She had no idea of the huge impact she would one day have on women and girls across the United States. She just wanted to contribute to her team by being the best soccer player she could be.

Ten years later, the best she could be is the best anyone has ever been. If the 1980s was colloquially known as the "Me" decade, the 1990s has so far been the "Mia" decade in the world of women's soccer. "Growing up a soccer fanatic, I could look at Mia and say 'There's a girl who loves the game as much as I do. . . . That's important. For a long time, my only soccer role models were men," one of her fans recently told a national reporter.

"Several words come to mind when talking about Mia, first and foremost being 'excitement,'" said U.S. Head Coach Tony DiCicco, who took over the national team reins from Anson Dorrance in 1994. "Just watching her play is a pleasure. What she does for the team as far as scoring goals, creating goals, and breaking down the defense is remarkable and

Focused in all situations, Mia Hamm dominates in a 1997 game vs. Germany, in which she scored 2 of the USA's 3 goals.

(Both photos: J. B. Whitesell, ISI)

helps the team accomplish its goals. When Mia is on, she makes you hold your breath."

Much has been written about the soccer prima donnas of the world—the players who run only with the ball, not without it. The players who give not so much interviews, but audiences to the media. The players who have little time for the fans. These are special players, who because they have the rare talent to score goals regularly put themselves above their coaches and teammates. Hamm has little in common with those players—though her haul includes 4 NCAA championships (for the University of North Carolina, where she was a political science major and she was nicknamed, "Jordan," after another alumnus who revolutionized his sport), 2 Hermann Awards, three USSF Soccer Athlete of the Year awards, a 1996 Olympic gold medal, and a 1991 World Cup–winners' medal (at age 19)—except her intense desire to decide a game and the talent to do exactly that.

"Coaching the best player in the world in some situations can be very, very difficult," said DiCicco, who now has a burden once shouldered by John Cossaboon in Texas, then by Anson Dorrance at the University of North Carolina and on the national team. "That player could have an arrogance and look down on her teammates. In my situation, it's not difficult as Mia is the consummate team player. She always defers all her accomplishments to her teammates. She came up to me after the Germany game [a 3–1 loss in October 1997 that broke the USA's 30-game unbeaten streak] and said to me, 'I've got to take on more responsibility, don't I?' That's the way she always approaches the game.

"She's just a joy to coach. She always wants to get better. She wants feedback from the coaching staff and the only thing I need to worry about is not inhibiting her from unleashing her incredible talents. So I try not to interfere with her creativity and still get her to play within the team structure."

With 80 goals in her first 134 international games, Hamm's scoring exploits are legendary, but it's the scope of her game that DiCicco enjoys the most.

"When I look at a player, I look at what special quality they have," he said. "Are they skillful? Are they athletic? Do they have a desire and a commitment to the game? Well, Mia has all those things. Everybody talks about Mia's attacking skills, but she's also one of the best defenders on the team."

"Once we've won the ball, she's one of the best dribblers in the world when it comes to taking players on. She'll get stopped once in a while, but through the course of a game, her defender is going to be victimized. She's a great finisher, an excellent passer, and she's a team player. When you mix all these things together, you don't have a good player, you don't have a very good player, you have a very, very special player, and that's why she carries the tag as the best in the world."

While still withdrawn in public—one of her favorite sayings, is from a letter Dorrance once wrote her after watching her train alone: "A champion is someone who is bending over to exhaustion when no one else is looking"—Hamm has matured during her 10 years in the spotlight and is now willing and able to cope with the demands and expectations that come with her unique fame, on and off the field.

"I think she has a growing feeling that she needs to make a play for the team," added DiCicco. "That's actually a wonderful quality to have, and I think we have a number of players on the U. S. team like that. But Mia just feels that if things aren't going well—or if they are going well, but we're just not sticking it in the back of the net—she's got to do something special. She wants to put fear in the opponent and make them lose a bit of confidence. If she has to, she'll just get it done herself. She knows that she's on the field to get that goal for the team. And all that is what separates the great ones. The ones that want the game on their shoulders."

At times, Hamm has been seen as distant, but DiCicco says that is part of the intense focus necessary to perform up to her own high standards—to deal with the wonderful burden of being the best that comes from her teammates, fans, opponents, and certainly herself.

"She's naturally shy, so basically one of the ways she prepares for games is to remove herself, not necessarily from her teammates, but from all the distractions," said DiCicco. "Before games, you'll see people yelling for her, trying to get her to wave to them and stuff, but she becomes so focused that I don't think she even hears them. She has to prepare every game for a physical beating. I don't know how else to say it nicely. I mean, they're going to try to stop her and stop her physically. She has to protect herself, but she can't be avoiding that aspect of the game because we need her to win balls and tackles and be strong and hold the ball for us up front. So to prepare for those types of games, I think she does have to remove herself a bit."

Through all the experience Hamm has acquired over the last 10 years, she seems poised to make the 1999 FIFA Women's World Cup her stage, to leave her mark on the tournament that makes soccer players into soccer legends.

"The most exciting thing about Mia Hamm," says DiCicco repeatedly, "is that she hasn't reached her peak yet." ⚽

Ever a target of rough defending, Mia Hamm's extraordinary skills include weathering the physical game as well as any player.
(J. B. Whitesell, ISI)

An American female soccer player will wear many uniforms in her career. She will don the colors of her youth league, club high school, state team, regional and college teams. If she is lucky, and lives in a populous area, she may now find a club team to play for after college. But only a select few get to wear the most coveted shirt of all—that of the U. S. Women's national team. The honor is in fact internationally referred to as being "capped," in reference to nineteenth-century soccer uniforms in which players competed in caps with their club or country's colors embroidered on them; these gradually became ceremonial and exclusively awarded for international appearances.

As captain of the 1996 Olympic champions, United States sweeper Carla Overbeck knows a bit about wearing her country's colors. She knows of the honor this holds and the responsibility entailed. She knows all of this from pulling on the uniform bearing her country's crest more than 100 times and walking single file with her teammates into a stadium to play for a dynasty, for that is what the American team is, consistently among the very best in the world.

"Not a lot people get to represent their country in the way that we do," said Overbeck, a 10-year veteran of the national team and in fact one of only seven U. S. female players to earn 100 or more caps. Among soccer players only a handful

160

TEAM USA
WITH CARLA OVERBECK

have earned that many caps; indeed, in any country in the world, players making 100 international appearances are unequivocally household names.

For the United States women players, there is a deep sense of reciprocity. Without exaggeration one might say they play with a sense of destiny. "When we're standing in a stadium, whether it be in China, or in Germany or even the United States, we're representing every American every time we step on the field." Overbeck has said. "We carry that with us every time we're with the national team or we're traveling as a team to foreign countries. It means something special and it's something none of us takes for granted."

"When you are playing for your country, there is a tremendous amount of pride," added Overbeck. "But it's a big responsibility. And in the last few years, we've had such a huge following among the youth soccer players. The little girls of America aspire to be like women's national team players; so on the field, you want to represent your country in a way that makes them proud.

"That pride in our team is not something that's spoken—it's just understood," she said of the bond between players.

"I've never really talked to anyone on the team about it, but there's a love for each other and our country there that's

unconditional. Everyone just plays for each other."

Recalling her debut with the national team, as a 19-year old, Overbeck says it took time to realize just how special an honor it is to play for your country." Back when I started, the national team trips were very limited, so you didn't really have a sense of how important it was," she remembered. "But the team has grown up together and as you mature and grow as a human being, you have a better understanding of pride and honor. The Olympics in 1996 were representative of the energy we've felt from the fans over the years. You really got an understanding of what playing for your country is about. Playing in front of 76,000 people in the U. S. was just incredible."

Overbeck received a special honor during the Olympic final as the game actually marked her 100th appearance for the U. S. national

team; for that moment to come at home, in a world championship final, one in which they hang gold medals around the winners' necks after the match, is the rarest honor of all.

"It was pretty cool," said Overbeck. "The 100th cap is a great achievement for any soccer player. Obviously, the 100th game is something you want to remember as a positive experience. And certainly playing in front of that many people, in the Olympic final and beating China, is a feeling and a day that I'm going to cherish for the rest of my life."

Overbeck plans to play through the 1999 Women's World Cup in the United States and then to make another run at Olympic gold in Sydney, Australia, in 2000. By then, she wants to make sure that those who come after her take as much pride in the national team shirt as her generation of women's soccer pioneers.

"I know women in other sports that came before us didn't get the recognition that they deserved like we're getting now," she said. "Obviously, they have paved the way for us. When I stop playing, I want to make sure that the young players know about the tradition and success of our team. I just want to feel comfortable when we leave that we're leaving the program in good hands.

"The federation is developing the Under-20s and the Under-16s so that they know what it takes to be on the women's team, to be the best and to work hard. We want to make sure that our mentality is implanted into the younger players to show them that it's not easy to be the best and to stay on top. Through our work and success we can make sure that to wear the national team jersey will always be something extra special to them."

That understanding of what it takes to be a champion has been learned over many games and thousands of practices. "When you're on the top team in the world, you're on the team to beat," said Overbeck, who was also a member of the USA's 1991 World Cup champions and of the third-place team at the 1995 World Cup. "The best quality about our team is that we're never satisfied with what we have. We all know that there are so many different ways that can personally improve and also improve as a team."

"Every time we step on the field, we know that teams are coming after us, and I sort of like it. Because as competitive as our team is, that's what we need, that's what makes us go. We love competition, we love playing tough teams. Every game we play we try to better ourselves and make women's soccer a sport that people want to watch in America, to make it fun for the fans as well. I know we have a great time when we're out there and we want the fans to enjoy it as much as we do."

So far, how can they not be. ⚽

Left: Tiffeny Milbrett, here in a 1995 World Cup finals game vs. Japan, scored the goal that beat China and clinched Olympic gold for the U. S. team.

Center: Wing half Kristine Lilly is the all-time appearance leader for the U. S. national team. Her 139 caps, the first when she was 16, is close to a record for all players; she has appeared in 85 percent of all U. S. national games ever.

Below: Brandi Chastain has been a team regular since the 1991 World Cup, in which USA beat France on the way to capturing the trophy.
(All photos: J. B. Whitesell, ISI)

Getting all ten men behind the ball, literally:
Brazil's wall stops France's Zidane threading
the ball into goal from a rare free kick in
the area (after the goalie had illegally
handled a back pass) in 1997
Tournoi de France action.
(Tempsport, Richiardi)

TACTICS
WITH STEVE SAMPSON
BY STEVE GOFF

The world has changed. Soccer has changed. The Iron Curtain came down, the Berlin Wall fell. The one-dimensional player is nearly extinct. Eastern Europe has shifted to the West, and the shackles on its wonderfully skilled players have been removed. The official sport of mankind and the blue planet has gradually evolved over the years, no more so than in its styles of play and tactics. Players are bigger, stronger, faster than ever before. Defenders score goals and forwards have begrudgingly learned how to play defense. Goalkeepers—yes, goalkeepers! —have become experts at dummying and passing and not only stopping the free kick, but even scoring that way, too.

Steve Sampson, coach of the U. S. men's national team, has observed the metamorphosis for several years—as a highly respected college coach at the University of Santa Clara, as a World Cup administrator, as an assistant to Bora Milutinovic for the 1993–1994 World Cup campaign, and, since 1995, as the official U. S. guide on the long, arduous trail to the 1998 World Cup in France.

He has seen changes around the world, and he has applied his own to the ever-evolving American squad. Just eight years ago, the United States was a world weakling in soccer—missing out on forty years's worth of World Cup finals. For decades, the U. S. team was shaped by an incoherent pool of naive college players, European and Hispanic immigrants, and suburban soccer boom graduates. But things have changed dramatically.

"In soccer, the United States was not physically nor technically proficient enough to compete with the best teams in the world until I'd say 1994," Sampson notes. "Through the 1990 World Cup, The American tactics in the modern era were a very conservative, very predictable defensive style. Anytime we attempted to break away from that, we were punished by the better teams. We were punished—quite frankly—because we just weren't good enough on the ball."

But things have changed. The American player has gained more international experience, has learned how to hold the ball under pressure, has absorbed the importance of even the slightest nuances of the game. The success of the national team in the 1994 World Cup and also in the 1995 Copa America demonstrated the progress of the American elite players.

It no longer was necessary to sit back and allow the opposition to dictate the game. American tactics had evolved to the point at which there no longer was an obvious mismatch on the field.

"It wasn't until we had players after the '90 World Cup go overseas and start gaining experience that we were capable of even *thinking* of playing the less conservative style, " Sampson explained. "Their experience, combined with the training and development program prior to the '94 World Cup in Mission Viejo, allowed us to be somewhat more competitive. Yet still the approach that Bora took during the World Cup was very position-oriented, a conservative style and conservative tactics that allowed us to stay in games. It wasn't one in which we were going to impose ourselves on the opposition.

"We would take advantage of certain situations in the game, but whenever we attacked it was always attack with the shape that if you lose possession of the ball, you don't get countered on.

"You can always get numbers behind the ball and that's what Bora worked on for two years. It's difficult for a coach to say, 'We're not good enough, guys, this is the way we're going to play.' He never said that; what he said was, 'The most important thing is position.' And it's true; but in order to *beat* the best in the world, it takes so much more than that."

So when Sampson became the interim coach in the spring of 1995, he decided it was time to move the U. S. squad ahead in a tactical sense. He knew it would be risky. He wondered if he had the proper personnel to accomplish his goals. But he also saw a new generation of players acquiring experience overseas—in the rigorous English league, in the Bundesliga, in Italy's Serie A, and in Mexico and Spain. It was time, he felt, to take a step up soccer's crowded ladder.

"It was very risky. I had nothing to lose," said Sampson. "No one expected me to succeed. But I think the players were ready for it. If not then, when? Plus, I wanted to begin to develop a blueprint for how we wanted all our teams to play. We're far from achieving that goal. But we're starting to."

Players such as Tab Ramos and Claudio Reyna were given the freedom to push the ball forward directly and go to the goal. Eric Wynalda had the green light to make a calculated run into empty space way upfield, knowing the ball would be delivered. The U. S. team welcomed the refreshing tactics with impressive results in the 1995 U.S. Cup and in Copa America.

Meanwhile, the rest of the world has changed, too. In Europe and in South America players became interchangeable, defenders became forward-moving sweepers, midfielders became defenders, forwards became playmakers. This new freedom inspired a number of experimental formations.

"You get no hesitation from a player to fill the space left by someone else," Sampson said. "The key was free-flowing interchange of positions as long as you kept your balance and shape defensively. That is the key. The Brazilians are the ones that have done the most in terms of allowing their players the freedom to move, yet recognize how to balance off each other."

Sampson also assessed the approach of the coach to the game's changes. "In the modern age of soccer you're playing a number of different systems with the game itself and really systems are out the window," Sampson said. "We can rename systems 'tendencies' in the team's approach to the game. What it comes down to is that you must observe the opposition's mobility. It becomes a chess match: how much risk do I take to force you to defend me? This is why the game is so complicated right now, because the way in which a team plays can be changed dramatically by the use of just one player on the field.

"We have made enormous strides. We have made incredible strides in part because we are Americans," he explained. "It's discipline, it's expectation, it's work ethic. It is ingrained in us that we can achieve things that no one else can. One day we will prove that in this sport. One day we will win a world championship. And you know why? Because Americans won't rest until they do. That mentality allows us to compete. It doesn't allow us not to beat the best. Americans will find ways to get better, they will find ways to win. Once we achieve what the rest of the world has, we will be a dominant force in this sport. Forever."

Right: Juggling game: Italy's superb roving playmaker Gianfranco Zola (formerly of Parma, now at Chelsea).
(Richiardi)

Opposite: Steve Sampson has coached the U. S. team with unprecedented success since 1995.
(J. B. Whitesell, ISI)

TACTICAL FORMATIONS

In an age when technical directors and specialized coaches are analyzing soccer in greater detail than ever, from player development to field strategy, with men such as Barcelona's Louis Van Gaal, A. C. Milan's Fabio Capello, and Juventus' Marcello Lippi in great demand the world over, the best coaches are still known as much for their leadership of men as their battlefield plans. Roy Hodgson, who has coached Internazionale Milan as well as overachievers Blackburn, Malmo, and Switzerland, is the archetypal believer in teamwork: "Everywhere you go, it's about your ability to get men to follow you as a leader. . .in sharing responsiblity around," he has said. But just *how* to share it has been the impetus for evolving tactics for the last 100 years.

2-3-5

For soccer's first 50 years it was assumed that the offense was the most important ingredient to every team. Players threw themselves instinctively into attack, but gradually it was understood that this left their own goal exposed to counteroffensives. The first tactical lineup was formed with three lines of players in front of the goalkeeper, who was called on—once the use of handling was allowed—as a specialist to guard the goal. (In the 1990s every effort has been made to bring the goalkeeper back into the field of play, as it were.) In this formation, players kept to their linear positions: there were two fullbacks, three halfbacks, five forwards. The center half (the central midfielder) marked the opposing center forward and was both the key playmaker and the pivot between offense and defense. Seen from above, this lineup appears to be a pyramid, and great emphasis was placed on holding the formation.

THE METHOD, OR MM

In the 1920s and 1930s, soccer strategy underwent distinct changes, with the increasing professionalization of the game leading to a generation of experienced coaches. In Europe, the Method, or MM formation, came into fashion. Two backs and two wing halfbacks lined up with a center half to delineate the first, more withdrawn M shape in front of the goalkeeper. The two wing halfs on either side of the three forwards formed the second, more advanced M. The Method emphasized teamwork, passing, and integrated movement on attack and defense; Uruguay and Italy won the first four World Cups using the Method. Austria's Wunderteam perfected its use, moving upfield in formation and playing short passes across the line of the M to keep possession.

THE SYSTEM, OR WM

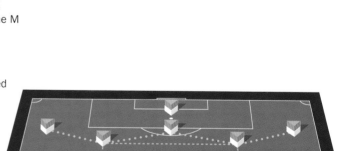

After World War II, the System, also known as WM, was developed to counter the strengths of the best Method teams. Anticipated by Herbert Chapman, coach of England's Arsenal club in the 1930s, this was really a variation of the Method. In front of the goalie there were now three defenders—the center half of the Method becoming a defender—spread across the field on the same line. In the midfield, two halfbacks and two wing halfs formed a quadrilateral and three forwards were aligned up front. Although the system was used widely, Uruguay still won the World Cup in 1950 by Method play, but with a player roaming the field diagonally looking to create turnovers and create counterattacks (see Method diagram above). For Uruguay that player was Schiaffino, the first great wing half playmaker.

THE HONVED MODEL

The Hungarian club Honved F. C. from Budapest—the source of the great Hungary teams of the 1950s— made an indelible mark on the game in the 1950s. The Honved Model, attributed to Gustav Sebes, vice minister of sport and coach of the national team, could be called WW. The defending line and the midfield line remain the same as in the System, but the forward line is reversed. The wings and the center forward are behind the inside forwards (the System's wing halfs), who now play in a more forward role than in the System. Wings and center forward provide the front line of forwards, rather than the reverse.

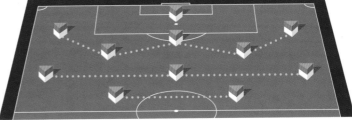

For the Honved team, Kocsis and Puskás played up front whereas the wings, Budai and Czibor, withdrew to the same line as the now withdrawn center forward, Hidegkuti, the first celebrated player who was able to use this deep-lying position to take defenders by surprise.

FROM THE SWEEPING GAME TO THE LIBERO

The 1950s saw the introduction of the epoch of excessive defense—best described as, "First, don't let in a goal, then take the enemy by surprise via the center forward." Although such play was not spectacular, it was often profitable for the Swiss national team and the Swiss club Servette Geneva, both coached by the Austrian Karl Rappan, who gave the name of this scheme to history: *verrou* in Swiss-German (*beton* in French, *catenaccio* in Italian, literally "bolt" in English). It was first practiced in Italy by Padova in 1941, and became popular in the 1950s. The marking of the opponents was tight—man to man— sometimes with help from an overlapping winger who could defend or move forward. But in the long run, this scheme did not pay off, and after the 1950s it was modified because of the need for better defense. There was always the risk that the center half, in line with the two backs, might be isolated in front of the opposing forwards: once past him, in fact, the center forward came face to face with the goalkeeper and therefore was in the best situation to score a goal. To prevent this, a libero—the free man, or "sweeper"—was necessary in front of the goalkeeper and behind the backs and center half, who in this scheme still marked the center forward and became the "stopper," in soccer terminology. The idea was to offer additional security to the defense. The sweeper formation has been popular among professional teams in most countries for decades, and three of the recent World Cups were won by teams playing in this formation: Italy in 1982 with Gaetano Scirea as sweeper; Argentina in 1986 with José-Luis Brown; and Germany in 1990 with Klaus Augenthaler. Franz Beckenbauer, who won the World Cup as a player in 1974, revolutionized the role in the 1970s by turning it into a position from which, when free of defensive responsibilities, attacks could first be mounted.

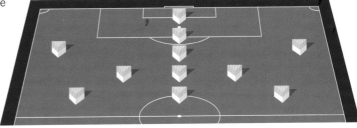

BY MAN—BY ZONE

Recently soccer tactics have undergone changes, often very short-lived, but the contrast between zone play and man-to-man play remains. The first change is a derivation of the Method, in which players are marked according to their position on the field and schemes are determined by the behavior of the opponent. Specific man-to-man markings are not used. There are two peculiar characteristics of zone play: the full press and the offside trap. Zone play takes a scientific approach to the offside trap; when the opponent attacks, the

defense moves up, causing the opponents to withdraw or risk being offside, as well as cutting off the opposing forwards. This means that the defensive phase begins practically at the same moment in which control of the ball is lost. Pressing—an aggressive attempt to move forward and control the opponent in possession of the ball—immediately takes place.

Most teams are now starting to play the zone system, and from experience most coaches maintain that the 4-4-2 arrangement is the most functional and profitable: four defenders in line (or almost), four midfielders in line (or almost), and two forwards. The most common variations are 4-3-3, with one midfielder becoming a forward or a winger who tries to spread the defense, or 4-2-4. But other schemes exist, the most effective of which was used a great deal in the 1990 World Cup in Italy, although the first to use it were the Belgian clubs Anderlecht and Malines. This scheme foresaw the sweeper behind or on line with the four defenders in the so-called "five-man defense," which was also used at Italia '90 by England, Germany, and Brazil. But three defenders can also play by zone with the sweeper behind, as shown by the 1990 Soviet team of Valeri Lobanovski.

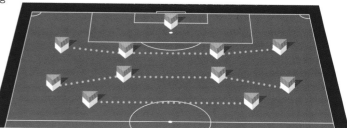

(pp. 168–170: diagrams by Brent Hatcher)

TEAMS IN MOTION

Today, following Brazil's 1994 World Cup triumph with a 4-4-2 formation, several international teams have retained the formation, reverted back to it, or maintained a zonal 5-3-2 variant. But even within 4-4-2, there tends to be a very broad variety of interpretation—most usually with the outside midfielders, often even the defenders, playing an overlapping, attacking role on the wing and with one midfielder supporting the forwards closely. The roving forward midfielder, sometimes considered a deep-lying forward, was a strategy used very successfully in Euro '96 and in the World Cup '98 qualifying rounds by several teams. The long-debated dispute between man-to-man and zone schemes has been diluted into a sort of mixed environment, where man-to-man marking progressively includes elements of zonal organization, mainly in the defensive scheme, while zonal play often requires hybrid forms of specific man-to-man guarding when the quality of the adversary requires it. Trying to catch a defense out while it is switching from one to the other can be as integral to a counterattack as breaking the offside trap. ⚽

England's offensive-minded 3-5-2 formation updates the classical 4-4-2.

4-4-2 masters Brazil now operate with a more complex sweeper and roving forward supporter (Leonardo).

USA's traditional 4-3-3 formation with sweeper.

Argentina's idiosyncratic, player-specific 4-3-3 variation.

Italy's 5-3-2 "Christmas Tree" formation encourages overall field coverage and defensive reinforcement

Germany's 3-3-2-2 floods the midfield and utilizes two classic inside forwards.

(Gazzetta dello Sport)

WORLD CUP AND NATIONAL STATISTICS

OVERALL WORLD CUP STATISTICS

	1930	1934	1938	1950	1954	1958	1962	1966	1970	1974	1978	1982	1986	1990	1994
Registered Nations	13	32	36	32	38	51	56	81	70	99	106	108	121	112	145
Nations in Qualifying Tournament	0	29	32	27	36	48	51	53	70	92	98	105	113	105	130
Nations in Finals	13	16	15	13	16	16	16	16	16	16	16	24	24	24	24
Venue	Uruguay	Italy	France	Brazil	Switzerland	Sweden	Chile	England	Mexico	Germany	Argentina	Spain	Mexico	Italy	USA
Matches Played in Finals	18	18	18	22	26	35	32	32	32	38	38	52	52	52	52
Total Players in Finals	189	208	210	192	233	241	252	254	270	264	277	396	414	413	428
Goals Scored	70	70	84	88	140	126	89	89	95	97	102	146	132	115	141
Team Goal Average	3.8	4.1	4.7	4	5.3	3.9	2.8	2.8	3	2.6	2.7	2.8	2.5	2.2	2.7
Penalties Awarded	2	4	3	3	7	8	8	8	4	8	14	10	16	18	15
Penalties Scored	1	3	2	3	7	7	8	8	4	6	12	8	12	13	15
Total Attendance	434,500	395,000	483,000	1,337,000	943,000	868,000	776,000	1,614,677	1,673,975	1,774,022	1,610,215	1,856,277	2,402,951	2,517,348	3,587,538
Average Game Attendance	24,138	23,235	26,833	60,772	36,270	24,800	24,250	50,458	52,311	46,684	42,374	33,967	46,211	48,411	68,991

OLYMPIC GAMES (1908–1996)

Year Gold	Silver	Bronze
1900 GREAT BRITAIN	France	Belgium
1904 CANADA	USA	USA
1908 GREAT BRITAIN	Denmark	Holland
1912 GREAT BRITAIN	Denmark	Holland
1920 BELGIUM	Spain	Holland
1924 URUGUAY	Switzerland	Sweden
1928 URUGUAY	Argentina	Italy
1936 ITALY	Austria	Norway
1948 SWEDEN	Yugoslavia	Denmark
1952 HUNGARY	Yugoslavia	Sweden
1956 USSR	Yugoslavia	Bulgaria
1960 YUGOSLAVIA	Denmark	Hungary
1964 HUNGARY	Czechoslovakia	East Germany
1968 HUNGARY	Bulgaria	Japan
1972 POLAND	Hungary	USSR and East Germany
1976 EAST GERMANY	Poland	USSR
1980 CZECHO-SLOVAKIA	East Germany	USSR
1984 FRANCE	Brazil	Yugoslavia
1988 USSR	Brazil	West Germany
1992 SPAIN	Poland	Ghana
1996 NIGERIA	Argentina	Brazil

Most goals scored in a single match: Sophus Nielsen (Den) 1908/10; Gottfried Fuchs (Ger) 1912/10.

Highest attendance: France–Brazil, 2–0, Rose Bowl, Pasadena, CA, 1984, 101,799 people.

THE AFRICAN NATIONS CHAMPIONSHIP (1957–1996)

Year	Winner	Runner-up
1957	EGYPT	Ethiopia
1959	EGYPT	Sudan
1962	ETHIOPIA	Egypt
1963	GHANA	Sudan
1965	GHANA	Tunisia
1968	CONGO KINSHASA	Ghana
1970	SUDAN	Ghana
1974	ZAIRE	Zambia
1976	MOROCCO	Guinea
1978	GHANA	Uganda
1980	NIGERIA	Algeria
1982	GHANA	Libya
1984	CAMEROON	Nigeria
1986	EGYPT	Cameroon
1988	CAMEROON	Nigeria
1990	ALGERIA	Nigeria
1992	IVORY COAST	Ghana
1994	NIGERIA	Zambia
1996	SO. AFRICA	Tunisia

THE ASIAN NATIONS CUP (1956–1996)

Year	Winner	Finalist
1956	SOUTH KOREA	Israel
1960	SOUTH KOREA	Israel
1964	ISRAEL	India
1968	IRAN	Burma
1972	IRAN	South Korea
1976	IRAN	Kuwait
1980	KUWAIT	South Korea
1984	SAUDI ARABIA	China
1988	SAUDI ARABIA	South Korea
1992	JAPAN	Saudi Arabia
1996	SAUDI ARABIA	UAE

CONCACAF NATIONS CHAMPIONSHIP (1941–1996)

Year	Winner	Runner-up
1941	COSTA RICA	El Salvador
1943	EL SALVADOR	Costa Rica
1946	COSTA RICA	Guatemala
1948	COSTA RICA	
1951	PANAMA	
1953	COSTA RICA	
1955	COSTA RICA	
1957	HAITI	Curaçao
1960	COSTA RICA	Netherlands Antilles
1961	COSTA RICA	El Salvador
1963	COSTA RICA	El Salvador
1965	MEXICO	Guatemala
1967	GUATEMALA	Mexico
1969	COSTA RICA	Guatemala
1971	MEXICO	Haiti
1973	HAITI	Trinidad & Tobago
1977	MEXICO	Haiti
1981	HONDURAS	El Salvador
1985	CANADA	Honduras
1989	COSTA RICA	U.S.A.
1991	U.S.A.	Honduras
1993	MEXICO	USA
1996	MEXICO	Brazil

Note: From 1941 to 1961, championship of CCCF (Confederacion Centroamericano y del Caribe de Fútbol); from 1963, championship of CONCACAF.

THE EUROPEAN NATIONS CHAMPIONSHIP
(Henry Delaunay Cup 1960–1996)

Year	Winner	Finalist
1960	SOVIET UNION	Yugoslavia
1964	SPAIN	Soviet Union
1968	ITALY	Yugoslavia
1972	WEST GERMANY	Soviet Union
1976	CZECHOSLOVAKIA	West Germany
1980	WEST GERMANY	Belgium
1984	FRANCE	Spain
1988	HOLLAND	Soviet Union
1992	DENMARK	Germany
1996	GERMANY	Czech Republic

THE SOUTH AMERICAN CHAMPIONSHIP (COPA AMERICA) (1916–1997)

Year	Winner	Runner-up
1916	URUGUAY	Argentina
1917	URUGUAY	Argentina
1919	BRAZIL	Uruguay
1920	URUGUAY	Argentina
1921	ARGENTINA	Brazil
1922	BRAZIL	Paraguay
1923	URUGUAY	Argentina
1924	URUGUAY	Argentina
1925	ARGENTINA	Brazil
1926	URUGUAY	Argentina
1927	ARGENTINA	Uruguay
1929	ARGENTINA	Paraguay
1935	URUGUAY	Argentina
1937	ARGENTINA	Brazil
1939	PERU	Uruguay
1941	ARGENTINA	Uruguay
1942	URUGUAY	Argentina
1945	ARGENTINA	Brazil
1946	ARGENTINA	Brazil
1947	ARGENTINA	Paraguay
1949	BRAZIL	Paraguay
1953	PARAGUAY	Brazil
1955	ARGENTINA	Chile
1956	URUGUAY	Chile
1957	ARGENTINA	Brazil
1959	ARGENTINA	Brazil
1959	URUGUAY	Argentina
1963	BOLIVIA	Paraguay
1967	URUGUAY	Argentina
1975	PERU	Colombia
1979	PARAGUAY	Chile
1983	URUGUAY	Brazil
1987	URUGUAY	Chile
1989	BRAZIL	Uruguay
1991	ARGENTINA	Brazil
1993	ARGENTINA	Mexico
1995	URUGUAY	Brazil
1997	BRAZIL	Bolivia

ALL-TIME RANKINGS
FIFA WORLD CUP
ALL-TIME RANKING TABLE

#	Team	Played	Won	Tied	Lost	Goals For	Goals Against	Total Points Scored	Uruguay 1930	Italy 1934	France 1938	Brazil 1950	Switzerland 1954	Sweden 1958	Chile 1962	England 1966	Mexico 1970	Germany 1974	Argentina 1978	Spain 1982	Mexico 1986	Italy 1990	USA 1994
1	Brazil	73	49	13	11	159	68	111	6	14	3	2	5	1	1	11	1	4	3	5	5	9	1
2	Germany	73	42	16	15	154	97	100		3	10		1	4	7	2	3	1	6	2	2	1	5
3	Italy	61	35	14	12	97	59	84		1	1	7	10		9	9	2	10	4	1	12	3	2
4	Argentina	52	26	9	17	90	65	61	2	9				13	10	5		8	1	11	1	2	10
5	England	41	18	12	11	55	38	48				8	6	11	8	1	8			6	8	4	
6	Spain	37	15	9	13	53	44	39		5		4			13	10			10	12	7	10	8
7	Russia	34	16	6	12	60	40	38						7	6	4	5			7	10	17	18
8	Uruguay	37	15	8	14	61	52	38	1			1	4		12	7	4	13			16	16	
9	Sweden	38	14	9	15	66	60	37		8	4	3		2			9	5	13			21	3
10	France	34	15	5	14	71	56	35	7	9	6		11	3		14			12	4	3		
11	Yugoslavia	33	14	7	12	55	42	35	4			5	7	5	4			7		16		5	
12	Hungary	32	15	3	14	87	57	33		6	2		2	10	5	6			15	14	18		
13	Poland	25	13	5	7	39	29	31			11							3	5	3	14		
14	Netherlands	25	11	6	8	43	29	28		9	14							2	2			15	7
15	Czechoslovakia	30	11	5	14	44	45	27		2	5		14	9	2		15			19		6	
16	Austria	26	12	2	12	40	43	26		4			3	15					7	8		18	
17	Belgium	29	9	4	16	37	53	22	11	15	13		12				10			10	4	11	11
18	Mexico	33	7	8	18	31	68	22	13			12	13	16	11	12	6		16		6		13
19	Chile	21	7	3	11	26	32	17	5			9			3	13		11		22			
20	Romania	17	6	4	7	26	29	16	8	12	9						10					12	6
21	Switzerland	22	6	3	13	33	51	15		7	7	6	8		16	16							15
22	Scotland	20	4	6	10	23	35	14					15	14				9	11	15	19	18	
23	Bulgaria	23	3	7	13	21	46	13							15	15	13	12			15		4
24	Portugal	9	6	0	3	19	12	12								3					17		
25	Northern Ireland	13	3	5	5	13	23	11						8						9	21		
26	Peru	15	4	3	8	19	31	11	10										8	20			
27	Paraguay	11	3	4	4	16	25	10	9			11		12							13		
28	Cameroon	11	3	4	4	11	21	10												17		7	22
29	USA	14	4	1	9	17	33	9	3	16		10										23	14
30	Ireland Republic	9	1	5	3	4	7	7														8	16
31	Denmark	4	3	0	1	10	6	6													9		
32	GDR	6	2	2	2	5	5	6										6					
33	Columbia	10	2	2	6	13	20	6							14							14	19
34	Wales	5	1	3	1	4	4	5						6									
35	Morocco	10	1	3	6	7	13	5									14				11		23
36	Algeria	6	2	1	3	6	10	5												13	22		
37	Nigeria	4	2	0	2	7	4	4															9
38	Saudi Arabia	4	2	0	2	5	6	4															12
39	Costa Rica	4	2	0	2	4	6	4														13	
40	Tunisia	3	1	1	1	3	2	3											13				
41	Norway	4	1	1	2	2	3	3			12												17
42	Korea DPR	4	1	1	2	2	3	3								8							
43	Cuba	3	1	1	1	5	12	3			8												
44	Korea Republic	11	0	3	8	9	34	3					16								20	22	20
45	Turkey	3	1	0	2	10	11	2					9										
46	Honduras	3	0	2	1	2	3	2												18			
47	Israel	3	0	2	1	1	3	2									12						
48	Egypt	4	0	2	2	3	6	2		13												20	
49	Kuwait	3	0	1	2	2	6	1												21			
50	Australia	3	0	1	2	0	5	1										14					
51	Iran	3	0	1	2	2	8	1											14				
52	Bolivia	6	0	1	5	1	20	1	12			13											21
53	Iraq	3	0	0	3	1	4	0													23		
54	Canada	3	0	0	3	0	5	0													24		
55	Neth. East Indies	1	0	0	1	0	6	0			15												
56	UAE	3	0	0	3	2	11	0														24	
57	New Zealand	3	0	0	3	2	12	0												24			
58	Greece	3	0	0	3	0	10	0															24
59	Haiti	3	0	0	3	2	14	0										15					
60	Zaire	3	0	0	3	0	14	0										16					
61	El Salvador	6	0	0	6	1	22	0									16			24			

HISTORICAL GOALS SCORED IN WORLD CUP FINALS COMPETITIONS

	Goalscorer	Match	Goal	Result	Venue
1st goal	Laurent (FRA)	France v. Mexico	1:0	4:1	Montevideo, 13.7.1930
100th goal	Schiavo(ITA)	Italy v. USA	5:1	7:1	Rome, 27.05.1934
500th goal	Collins(SCO)	Paraguay v. Scotland	3:2	3:2	Norrköping, 11.06.1958
1000th goal	Resenbrink(HOL)	Scotland v. Netherlands	0:1	3:2	Mendoza, 11.06.1978
1500th goal	Caniggia(ARG)	Argentina v. Nigeria	1:1	2:1	Boston, 24.06.1994
1584th goal	Andersson(SWE)	Sweden v. Bulgaria	4:0	4:0	Los Angeles , 16.07.1994

* Penalty shootout goals not included

WORLD CUP FINALS INDIVIDUAL GOAL-SCORING RECORDS

GOALS

14	Gerd Müller	Germany	1970/10	1974/4
13	Just Fontaine	France	1958/13	
12	Pelé	Brazil	1958/6	1962/1
			1966/1	1970/4
11	Sandor Kocsis	Hungary	1954/11	
10	Helmut Rahn	Germany	1954/4	1958/6
	Teofilo Cubillas	Peru	1970/5	1978/5
	Grzegorz Lato	Poland	1974/7 1982/1	1978/2
	Gary Lineker	England	1986/6	1990/4
9	Leonidas	Brazil	1934/1	1938/8
	Ademir	Brazil	1950/9	
	Vava	Brazil	1958/5	1962/4
	Uwe Seeler	Germany	1958/2 1966/2	1962/2 1970-3
	Eusebio	Portugal	1966/9	
	Jairzinho	Brazil	1970/7	1974/2
	Paolo Rossi	Italy	1978/3	1982/6
	Karl-Heinz Rummenigge	Germany	1978/3 1986/1	1982/5
8	Guillermo Stabile	Argentina	1930/8	
	Diego Maradona	Argentina	1982/2 1994/2	1986/5
	Oscar Miguez	Uruguay	1950/5	1954/3
	Rudi Völler	Germany	1986/3 1994/2	1990/3
	Jürgen Klinsmann	Germany	1994/5	1990/3
7	Gyula Zsengeller	Hungary	1938/7	
	Hans Schäfer	Germany	1954/4	1958/3
	Lajos Tichy	Hungary	1958/4	1962/3
	Johnny Rep	Netherlands	1974/4	1978/3
	Andrzej Szarmach	Poland	1974/5 1982/1	1978/1
	Careca	Brazil	1986/5	1990/2
	Roberto Baggio	Italy	1990/2	1994/5
6	Oldrich Nejedly	Czechoslovakia	1934/4	1938/2
	Max Morlock	Germany	1954/6	
	Erich Probst	Austria	1954/6	
	Valentin Ivanov	USSR	1958/2	
	Helmut Haller	Germany	1966/6	
	Rivelino	Brazil	1970/3	1974/3
	Rob Rensenbrink	Netherlands	1974/1	1978/5
	Mario Kempes	Argentina	1978/6	
	Zbigniev Boniek	Poland	1978/2	1982/4
	Lothar Matthäus	Germany	1986/1 1994/1	1990/4
	Salvatore Schillaci	Italy	1990/6	
	Oleg Salenko	Russia	1994/6	
	Hristo Stoichkov	Bulgaria	1994/6	

USA MEN'S NATIONAL TEAM ALL-TIME LEADERS

APPEARANCES

	Name	Caps	Goals	Era
1.	Balboa, Marcelo	123	12	1988–present
2.	Caligiuri, Paul	114	5	1984–present
3.	Jones, Cobi	96	8	1992–present
4.	Murray, Bruce	93	21	1985–1993
5.	Lalas, Alexi	91	9	1990–present
6.	Wynalda, Eric	90	31	1990–present
7.	Meola, Tony	89	0	1988–1994
8.	Armstrong, Desmond	84	0	1987–1994
9.	Harkes, John	83	6	1987–present
10.	Perez, Hugo	79	16	1984–1994
11.	Ramos, Tab	77	6	1988–present
12.	Agoos, Jeff	76	3	1988–present
	Henderson, Chris	76	3	1990–present
14.	Dooley, Thomas	72	7	1992–present
	Vermes, Peter	72	11	1988–present

USA GOAL SCORERS

	Name	Goals	Caps	Era
1.	Wynalda, Eric	31	90	1990–present
2.	Murray, Bruce	21	93	1985–1993
3.	Perez, Hugo	16	79	1984–1994
	Moore, Joe-Max	16	58	1992–present
5.	Klopas, Frank	13	45	1987–1996
6.	Davis, Rick	12	49	1977–1988
	Balboa, Marcelo	12	123	1988–present
8.	Vermes, Peter	11	72	1988–present
9.	Kinnear, Dominic	10	55	1990–1995
10.	Murphy, Eddie	9	24	1955–1969
	Lalas, Alexi	9	91	1989–present
12.	Jones, Cobi	8	96	1992–present
13.	Roy, Willy	7	20	1965–1973
	Goulet, Brent	7	17	1986–1990
	Thomas Dooley	7	72	1992–present

USA ASSISTS RECORDS

	Name	Assists	Caps	Era
1.	Ramos, Tab	14	77	1988–present
2.	Jones, Cobi	12	96	1992–present
3.	Harkes, John	11	83	1987–present
	Wynalda, Eric	11	90	1990–present
5.	Henderson, Chris	10	76	1990–present
	Lalas, Alexi	10	91	1989–present
7.	Moore, Joe-Max	8	58	1992–present
	Reyna, Claudio	8	53	1994–present
	Perez, Hugo	8	79	1984–1994
10.	Wegerle, Roy	7	29	1992–present
11.	Burns, Mike	6	61	1992–present
	Michallik, Janusz	6	44	1991–1994
	Murray, Bruce	6	93	1985–1993
14.	Balboa, Marcelo	4	123	1988–present
	Caligiuri, Paul	4	114	1984–present
	Stewart, Ernie	4	42	1990–present

USA GOALKEEPER RECORDS: APPEARANCES

	Names	Caps	Starts	Era
1.	Meola, Tony	89	87	1988–1994
2.	Friedel, Brad	53	52	1992–present
3.	Mausser, Arnie	35	32	1975–1983
4.	Keller, Kasey	25	24	1990–present
5.	Vanole, David	24	24	1986–1989

USA GOALKEEPER WINS

	Names	Wins	Caps	Era
1.	Meola, Tony	31	89	1988–1994
2.	Keller, Kasey	15	25	1990–present
3.	Friedel, Brad	12	53	1992–present
4.	Vanole, David	9	24	1986–1989
5.	Mausser, Arnie	7	35	1975–1983

USA GOALKEEPER SHUTOUTS

	Names	SO	Caps	Era
1.	Meola, Tony	27	89	1988–1994
2.	Friedel, Brad	13	53	1992–present
3.	Keller, Kasey	10	25	1990–present
	Mausser, Arnie	10	35	1975–1983
5.	Dodd, Mark	7	15	1988–present
	Vanole, David	7	24	1986–1989

USA MEN'S NATIONAL TEAM ALL-TIME RECORDS

Most consecutive wins overall

4 (four times)
- 12/2/79–3/20/80
- 6/16/87–10/18/87
- 6/29/91–7/5/91
- 7/10/93–7/21/93

Most consecutive wins in the USA

4 (two times)
- 6/29/91–7/5/91
- 7/10/93–7/21/93

Most consecutive wins outside the USA

3; 6/16/87–10/18/87

Most consecutive games unbeaten overall

9 (two times)
- 12/2/79–10/25/80
- 6/1/91–7/14/91

Most consecutive losses overall

12; 5/27/34–9/4/49

Most consecutive losses in the USA

5; 6/19/49–5/28/59

Most consecutive losses outside the USA

14; 10/16/73–8/28/75

*USA Records as of 2/1/98

USA MEN'S MATCH RECORDS

Most goals scored
8; 11/14/93, USA 8, Cayman Islands 1

Most goals scored in defeat
3 (four times)
- 8/17/30, USA 3, Brazil 4
- 9/19/37, USA 3, Mexico 7
- 6/8/53, USA 3, England 6
- 6/13/93, USA 3, Germany 4

Most goals allowed
11 (twice)
- 5/30/28, USA 2, Argentina 11
- 8/6/48, USA 0 Norway 11

Most goals allowed in win
3 (twice)
- 10/20/68, USA 6, Haiti 3
- 10/8/95, USA 4, Saudi Arabia 3

Most goals for both teams
13; 5/20/28, USA 2, Argentina 11

Largest margin of victory
7 (twice)
- 11/14/93, USA 8, Cayman Islands 1
- 12/5/93, USA 7, El Salvador 0

Largest margin of victory, shutout
7; 12/5/93, USA 7, El Salvador 0

Largest margin of defeat
11; 8/6/48, USA 0 Norway 11

Largest margin of defeat, shutout
11; 8/6/48, USA 0 Norway 11

SEASON RECORDS

Most international matches played
34; 1993

Fewest international matches played
0; 27 different years

Most wins
10; 1993

Most losses
14; 1990

Most ties
11; 1993

Most consecutive wins
4 (two times); 1987, 1991

Most consecutive losses
6; 1975

USA MEN'S NATIONAL TEAM INDIVIDUAL RECORDS

MATCH RECORDS

Most goals
4; Archie Stark, 11/8/25 vs. Canada
4; Aldo "Buff" Donelli, 5/24/34 vs. Mexico
4; Joe-Max Moore, 12/5/93 vs. El Salvador

Most assists*
3, Cobi Jones, 11/14/93 vs. Cayman Islands

Most points*
10, Joe-Max Moore, 12/5/95 vs. El Salvador
(4 goals, 2 assists)

CAREER RECORDS

Most consecutive games played
30; Marcelo Balboa, 10/19/91–3/14/93

Most consecutive starts
30; Marcelo Balboa, 10/19/91– 3/14/93

Most consecutive games scoring a goal
4; William Looby, 1/14/54–8/25/55

Most consecutive games scoring an assist
3; Eric Wynalda, 6/29/91–7/3/91

* Assists and points are from 1990–present only.

USA MEN'S NATIONAL TEAM YEAR-BY-YEAR RECORDS

Year	GP	W	L	T	GF	GA
1916	2	1	0	1	4	3
1924	4	2	2	0	5	8
1925	2	1	1	0	6	2
1926	1	1	0	0	6	1
1928	2	0	1	1	5	14
1930	4	2	2	0	10	10
1934	2	1	1	0	5	9
1936	1	0	1	0	0	1
1937	3	0	3	0	6	19
1947	2	0	2	0	2	10
1948	3	0	3	0	0	25
1949	5	1	3	1	8	19
1950	3	1	2	0	4	8
1952	2	0	2	0	0	14
1953	1	0	1	0	3	6
1954	4	2	2	0	7	9
1955	1	0	1	0	2	3
1956	1	0	1	0	1	9
1957	4	0	4	0	5	21
1959	3	0	2	1	2	11
1960	2	0	1	1	3	6
1961	1	0	1	0	0	2
1963	4	0	4	0	3	30
1964	4	1	3	0	5	15
1965	4	1	1	2	4	5
1967	2	0	1	1	1	2
1968	9	4	4	1	22	22
1969	2	0	2	0	0	3
1971	5	2	0	3	9	4
1972	13	2	6	5	16	37
1973	12	3	9	0	5	22
1974	2	0	2	0	1	4
1975	10	1	9	0	7	47
1976	8	1	2	5	3	7
1977	8	3	3	2	7	11
1978	3	0	2	1	0	3
1979	*11	6	5	0	17	20
1980	10	4	3	3	13	15
1982	1	1	0	0	2	1
1983	1	1	0	0	2	0
1984	12	4	3	5	15	11
1985	8	2	3	3	6	12
1986	2	0	0	2	1	1
1987	8	5	3	0	14	9
1988	19	4	10	5	18	26
1989	12	6	3	3	12	7
1990	24	8	13	3	29	34
1991	18	8	5	5	22	15
1992	21	6	11	4	21	27
1993	34	10	13	11	45	44
1994	27	7	9	11	30	28
1995	14	5	6	3	20	18
1996	16	10	4	2	28	19
1997	18	5	6	7	22	21
Totals	395	122	181	92	484	709

* The USA won its final two qualification matches in 1979 against Mexico by forfeit because Mexico fielded ineligible players.

USA WOMEN'S NATIONAL TEAM ALL-TIME LEADERS

APPEARANCES

	Name	Caps	Goals	Era
1.	Lilly, Kristine	139	53	1987–present
2.	Hamm, Mia	136	81	1987–present
3.	Gabarra, Carin (Jennings)	117	53	1987–present
4.	Foudy, Julie	142	11	988–present
5.	Akers, Michelle	111	93	1985–present
6.	Overbeck, Carla	105	71	988–present
7.	Fawcett, Joy (Biefeld)	102	15	1987–present
8.	Venturini, Tisha	88	32	1992–present
9.	Milbrett, Tiffeny	82	33	1991–present
10.	Hamilton, Linda	71	0	1987–1995
11.	Scurry, Briana	59	0	1994–present
12.	Roberts, Tiffany	57	6	1994–present
13.	Chastain, Brandi	55	11	1988–present
14.	Cromwell, Amanda	52	1	1991–present
	Staples, Thori	52	0	1993–present
16.	Higgins, Shannon	51	4	1987–1991
17.	Belkin, Debbie	50	2	1986–1991
18.	Heinrichs, April	47	38	1986–1991
19.	McCarthy, Megan	42	0	1987–1994
20.	Henry, Lori	39	3	1985–1991
	MacMillan, Shannon	39	13	1993–present

USA WOMEN'S GOAL SCORERS

	Name	Goals	Caps	Era
1.	Akers, Michelle	93	111	1985–present
2.	Hamm, Mia	81	136	1987–present
3.	Lilly, Kristine	53	139	1987–present
	Gabarra, Carin (Jennings)	53	117	1987–present
5.	Heinrichs, April	37	47	1986–1991
6.	Milbrett, Tiffeny	33	82	1991–present
7.	Venturini, Tisha	32	88	1992–present
8.	Foudy, Julie	21	114	1988–present
9.	Fawcett, Joy	15	102	1987–present
10.	Parlow, Cindy	14	29	1996–present
11.	MacMillan, Shannon	13	39	1993–present
12.	Chastain, Brandi	11	55	1988–present
13.	Rafanelli, Sarah	8	34	1992–1996
14.	Overbeck, Carla	7	105	1988–present
15.	Roberts, Tiffany	6	57	1994–present

USA WOMEN'S ASSISTS

	Name	Assists	Caps	Era
1.	Hamm, Mia	56	136	1987–present
	Gabarra, Carin (Jennings)	49	117	1987–present
3.	Lilly, Kristine	41	139	1987–present
	Akers, Michelle	33	111	1985–present
5.	Foudy, Julie	24	114	1988–present
6.	Milbrett, Tiffeny	23	82	1991–present
7.	Venturini, Tisha	14	88	1992–present
8.	MacMillan, Shannon	12	39	1993–present
9.	Chastain, Brandi	11	55	1988–present
10.	Fawcett, Joy	10	102	1987–present
	Heinrichs, April	10	47	1986–1991

USA WOMEN'S GOALKEEPERS

APPEARANCES

	Names	Caps	Starts	Era
1.	Scurry, Briana	59	58	1994–present
2.	Harvey, Mary	27	25	1989–1996
3.	Allman, Amy	24	23	1987–1991
4.	Webber, Saskia	19	18	1992–1995

WINS

	Names	Wins	Caps	Era
1.	Scurry, Briana	47	59	1994–present
2.	Harvey, Mary	20	27	1989–1996
3.	Webber, Saskia	13	19	1992–1995
4.	Allman, Amy	12	24	1987–1991

SHUTOUTS

	Names	SO	Caps	Era
1.	Scurry, Briana	31	59	1994–present
2.	Harvey, Mary	13	27	1989–1996
3.	Allman, Amy	10	24	1987–1991
4.	Maslin-Kammerdeiner, Kim	9		1988–1991
	Webber, Saskia	9	19	1992–1995

USA WOMEN'S NATIONAL TEAM–TEAM RECORDS

ALL-TIME RECORDS

Most consecutive wins (overall)

18; 7/25/90–5/25/91

Most consecutive wins (in the USA)

19; 4/10/93–8/6/95

Most consecutive wins (outside the USA)

15; 7/25/90–5/25/91

Most consecutive games unbeaten (overall)

30; 2/10/96–10/9/97

Most consecutive losses (overall)

3 (twice)
- 8/30/91–10/4/91
- 3/12/93–4/7/93

Most consecutive losses (in the USA)

3; 8/30/91–10/4/91

Most consecutive losses (outside the USA)

2 (four times)

MATCH RECORDS

Most goals scored

12 (twice)
- 4/18/91, USA 12, Mexico 0
- 4/20/91, USA 12, Martinique 0

Most goals scored, defeat

3; 5/28/91, USA 3, Holland 4

Most goals allowed

4 (twice)
- 5/2/8/91, USA 3, Holland 4
- 8/16/92, USA 2, Norway 4

Most goals allowed, win

2 (11 times)

Most goals both teams

12 (three times)
- 4/18/91, USA 12, Mexico 0
- 4/20/91, USA 12, Martinique 0
- 8/17/94, USA 11, Trinidad & Tobago 1

Highest Scoring Tie

3-3 (twice)
- 3/19/95, USA 3, Norway 3
- 6/6/95, USA 3, China 3

Largest margin of victory

12 (twice)
- 4/18/91, USA 12, Mexico 0
- 4/20/91, USA 12, Martinique 0

Largest margin of victory, shutout

12 (twice)
- 4/18/91, USA 12, Mexico 0
- 4/20/91, USA 12, Martinique 0

Largest margin of defeat

2 (six times)

Largest margin of defeat, shutout

2 (twice)
- 7/27/88, USA 0, England 2
- 3/17/95, USA 0, Denmark 2

SEASON RECORDS

Most international matches played

28; 1991

Fewest international matches played

1; 1989

Most wins

21 (twice); 1991 and 1996

Most losses

6; 1991

Most ties

2 (three times); 1988, 1995 and 1996

Most consecutive wins

15; 1996

Most consecutive losses

3 (twice); 1991 and 1993

USA WOMEN'S NATIONAL TEAM INDIVIDUAL RECORDS

MATCH RECORDS

Most goals

5; Brandi Chastain, 4/18/91 vs. Mexico
5; Michelle Akers, 11/24/91 vs. Taiwan

Most assists

5; Tiffeny Milbrett, 6/5/97 vs. Australia

Most points

10; Mia Hamm (twice)
- 8/17/94 vs. Trinidad & Tobago (4 goals, 2 assists)
- 4/28/96 vs. France (4 goals, 2 assists)

CAREER RECORDS

Most consecutive games played

63; Carla Overbeck, 8/4/93–present

Most consecutive starts

41; Carla Overbeck, 84/93–1/16/96

Most consecutive games scoring a goal

9; Michelle Akers, 4/5/91–5/25/91

Most consecutive games scoring an assist

4; Michelle Akers, 8/13/94–8/21/94

USA WOMEN'S NATIONAL TEAM YEAR-BY-YEAR RECORDS

Year	GP	W	L	T	GF	GA
1985	4	0	3	1	3	7
1986	7	5	2	0	13	6
1987	11	6	4	1	23	9
1988	8	3	3	2	10	9
1989	1	0	0	1	0	0
1990	6	6	0	0	26	3
1991	28	21	6	1	122	22
1992	2	0	2	0	3	7
1993	17	13	4	0	54	7
1994	13	12	1	0	59	6
1995	23	19	2	2	82	16
1996	24	21	1	2	80	17
1997	18	16	2	0	67	13
Total	162	122	30	10	542	122

1998 FIFA WORLD CUP FINAL COMPETITION GAME SCHEDULE

	Group A	Group B	Group C	Group D	Group E	Group F	Group G	Group H
	Brazil **Scotland** **Morocco** **Norway**	**Italy** **Chile** **Cameroon** **Austria**	**France** **South Africa** **Saudi Arabia** **Denmark**	**Spain** **Nigeria** **Paraguay** **Bulgaria**	**Holland** **Belgium** **South Korea** **Mexico**	**Germany** **United States** **Yugoslavia** **Iran**	**Romania** **Colombia** **England** **Tunisia**	**Argentina** **Japan** **Jamaica** **Croatia**
June 10–15	Brazil–Scotland Saint-Denis Morocco–Norway Montpellier	Cameroon–Austria Toulouse Italy–Chile Bordeaux	Saudi Arabia–Denmark Lenz France–South Africa Marseilles	Paraguay–Bulgaria Montpellier Spain-Nigeria Nantes	Holland–Belgium Saint-Denis South Korea–Mexico Lyons	Yugoslavia–Iran St. Etienne Germany–United States Paris	Romania–Colombia Lyons England–Tunisia Marseilles	Jamaica–Croatia Lenz Argentina–Japan Toulouse
June 16–22	Scotland–Norway Bordeaux Brazil–Morocco Nantes	Chile–Austria St. Etienne Italy–Cameroon Montpellier	France–Saudi Arabia Saint-Denis South Africa–Denmark Toulouse	Nigeria–Bulgaria Paris Spain–Paraguay St. Etienne	Holland–South Korea Marseilles Belgium–Mexico Bordeaux	Germany–Yugoslavia Lenz United States–Iran Lyons	Colombia–Tunisia Montpellier Romania–England Toulouse	Japan–Croatia Nantes Argentina–Jamaica Paris
June 23–26	Scotland–Morocco St. Etienne Brazil–Norway Marseilles	Italy–Austria Saint Denis Chile–Cameroon Nantes	France–Denmark Lyons South Africa–Saudi Arabia Bordeaux	Spain–Bulgaria Lenz Nigeria–Paraguay Toulouse	Belgium–South Korea Paris Holland–Mexico St. Etienne	Germany–Iran Montpellier Yugoslavia–United States Nantes	Romania–Tunisia Saint-Denis Colombia–England Lenz	Japan–Jamaica Lyons Argentina–Croatia Bordeaux

Round of 16 | | | | | Quarterfinals |

June 27	**June 28**	**June 29**	**June 30**	**July 3**	**July 4**
1A–2B Paris	1C–2D Lenz	1E–2F Toulouse	1G–2H Bordeaux	W1–W4 Nantes	W5–W8 Marseilles
1B–2A Marseilles	1D–2C Saint-Denis	1F–2E Montpellier	1H–2G St. Etienne	W2–W3 Saint-Denis	W6–W7 Lyons

Semifinals | | Third and Fourth Places | | Final |

July 7		**July 11**	**July 12**
WA–WC Marseilles	WB–WD Saint-Denis	LA–C—LB–D Paris	WA–C—WB–D Saint-Denis

Reaching to their limits, young Ajax Amsterdam apprentice players fish for their ball.
(Allsport).

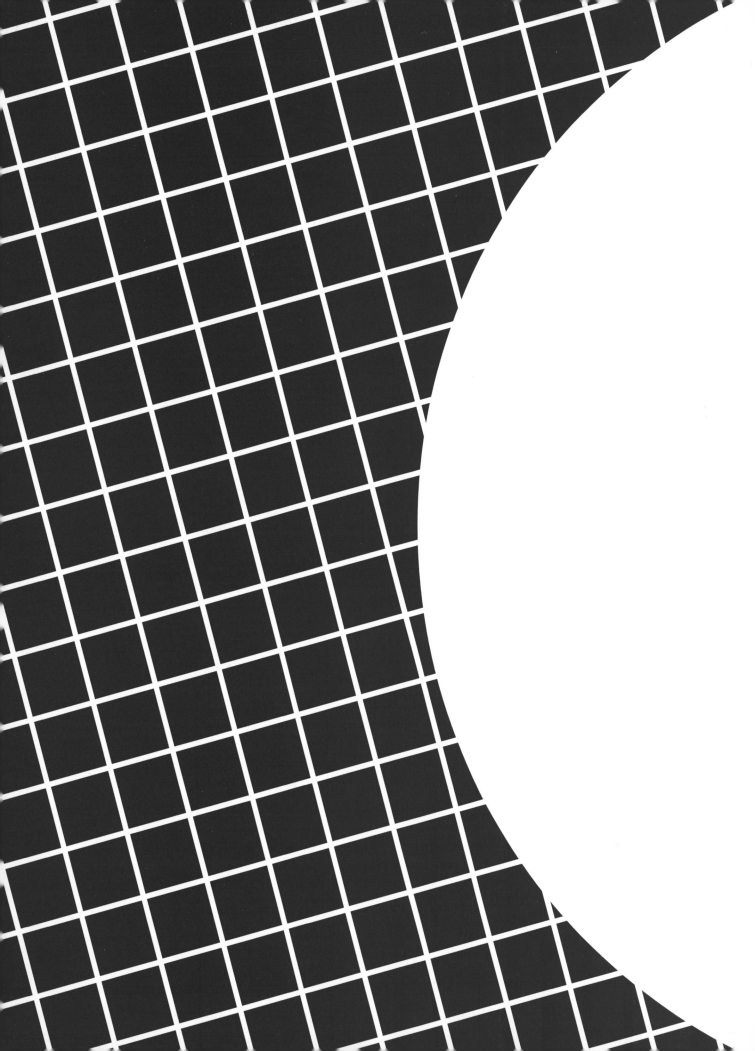